# Paroled but not Free

# PAROLED BUT NOT FREE

by
Rosemary J. Erickson, Wayman J. Crow
Louis A. Zurcher, Jr., and Archie V. Connett

Behavioral Publications          New York
1973

Library of Congress Catalog Number 73-4039

Standard Book Number
   Cloth—87705-095-3
   Paper—87705-109-7

BEHAVIORAL PUBLICATIONS, 2852 Broadway, Morningside Heights,
New York, New York 10025

Printed in the United States of America

This printing 10 9 8 7 6 5 4 3 2 1


**Library of Congress Cataloging in Publication Data**

Main entry under title.

Paroled but not free.

   Bibliography:  p.
   1.  Parole--California.   2.  Rehabilitation of
criminals--California.   I.  Erickson, Rosemary J.
HV9305.C2P33          364.6'2'09794          73-4039
ISBN 0-87705-095-3
ISBN 0-87705-109-7  (pbk)

Therefore, if you are in an attitude
of moral superiority to our convicts:
if you are one of the Serve Them Right
and Give Them Hell brigade, you may
justly be invited, in your own vernacular,
either to Come Off It, or else Go Inside
and take the measure you are meting out
to others no worse than yourself.

George Bernard Shaw in
*The Crime of Imprisonment*

# CONTENTS

# LIST OF TABLES

# PREFACE

This book describes the experience of being released from prison on parole. In the conduct of the study and in the presentation of this report, we have had two main objectives: (1) to obtain and present the perspective of the men who have lived through that experience, and (2) to demonstrate a style of behavioral science inquiry which we recommend to those who seek an increased contribution from science to the resolution of social problems. Most people would agree that it is unwise to make plans for the reform of prisons from the perspective of superintendents and wardens without including the perspective of prisoners; to reform courts from the perspective of judges and district attorneys without including the views of the accused; to reform parole without including input from parolees; or to conduct research from the perspective of academic disciplines without including the perspective of the ex-offender.

In a strange way sociological research has, however, excluded the ex-offender from consideration. Certainly he has been the object of concern—the subject of study—but rarely has he been included. The significance of the research that is reported here lies not only in the substantive results obtained, but also in the methods we used to include the ex-offender and the practitioner in the research team.

The purpose of this study was to use ex-offenders as the primary resource in determining what parolees believe to be their rehabilitation needs. This is not to say that the offender's perspective is the only "true" perspective but rather that it should be added to those of the professional, practitioner, and researcher in guiding the design of rehabilitation programs.

To improve communication and coordination of effort and to benefit fully from their input, selected representatives (key persons) from seventeen agencies or groups were invited to participate in a collaborative planning approach to this study, i.e., California Department of Corrections, California Department of Rehabilitation, California Youth Authority, Sheriff's Department, San Diego State College, as well as offenders, policemen, county judges, volunteers, and members of the minority community. Through collaborative planning seminars, the multiple perspectives of these stakeholders were focused on the design of the study, the selection of questions, and the interpretation of results. And, finally, they made recommendations based on the results.

We searched extensively to find other studies where the ex-offender's perspective was fully brought to bear upon these problems and did not locate any such study. So, for what may be the first time, information has been gathered systematically from ex-convicts by ex-convicts about how the parolee views his needs.

The emphasis of the research was upon determining the needs of the offender as he perceives them and only then relating these findings to general known theory. The book is arranged as the study was conducted. That is, the parolees' stories are presented first, in their own words, and then suggestions for relating their ideas to theoretical perspectives are made. The practitioners' recommendations are included, as are those of the offender. A unique epilogue by a successful ex-convict on the WBSI staff closes the book.

The results of this study have had an impact. A program designed to meet the needs revealed has been designed and began operation in September, 1972. It, too, is a collaborative effort among ex-offenders, the California Department of Corrections, the California State Department of Rehabilitation and Western Behavioral Sciences Institute. The study and the collaborative interaction also contributed to the formation of a coalition of private agencies providing services to ex-convicts which is bringing about greater coordination in their efforts. The study spurred efforts to establish Ex-Offender Resources, Inc., a non-profit organization of ex-convicts dedicated to achieving an improved system of criminal justice.

These steps are modest in relation to the need but nonetheless real. We recommend the style and the spirit of collaborative research.                                    W. J. CROW

# ACKNOWLEDGEMENTS

The parolees, whose interviews and comments are contained within this book, made this study possible. Our interviewers— Alex Kirach, Tony Raygosa, Tom Scott, Robert Tipton, Lee Turner and William Van Sneeden—were also ex-convicts.

The parole agents and many professionals in the field of corrections and rehabilitation, along with the ex-convicts, participated in various ways throughout the study. We owe special thanks to Ray Johnson and Robert McKinney, Ex-Offender Resources, Inc.; Mr. Paul Cossette, District Administrator of Parole and Community Services Division, California Department of Corrections; Christopher Minard, District Administrator, California Department of Rehabilitation; Eugene Bischoff and Don Sayre, California Department of Rehabilitation.

Portions of this study were presented as a thesis—"The Ex-Offender Looks At His Own Needs" by Rosemary J. Erickson —for completion of the Master of Arts Degree in Sociology at San Diego State College, under the direction of Drs. Aubrey Wendling, G. Thomas Gitchoff, and Robert W. Winslow.

This investigation was supported in part by Research and Demonstration Grant No. 15-P-55287/9, from the Division of Research and Demonstration Grants, Social and Rehabilitation Service, Department of Health, Education, and Welfare, Washington, D. C. 20201. The final report submitted March 31, 1971, was *The Offender Looks At His Own Needs*, by Rosemary J. Erickson, Wayman J. Crow, Louis A. Zurcher, Archie V. Connett, and William D. Stillwell. Additional funds for the study were contributed by Western Behavioral Sciences Institute.

Several members of the staff at Western Behavioral Sciences Institute were invaluable to the completion of the study, especially Jessie Rohrbough who provided the editorial assistance.

Chapter 1

# The Parolees Tell Their Own Stories

One-half of all prisoners released may eventually return to prison, a fact strongly suggesting that our prisons do not rehabilitate a satisfactory proportion of their inmates. Since the cost of incarceration is about ten times as much as supervision on parole, the costs of recidivism, both economic and social, are immense. One of the most important developments in twentieth century corrections may be the facilitating of the transition from prison confinement to functional freedom (Glaser, 1972). This book is about 60 men experiencing that transition.

The purpose of the research was to use parolees themselves as the primary source for learning about the rehabilitation needs of ex-offenders when they are released from prison. In order to accomplish that objective, 6 ex-offenders were trained in interviewing techniques; they then interviewed a sample of 60 adult males who were on parole in San Diego County. One-half of the sample was drawn from among all adult male felons on parole in August of 1970. The remaining 30 were selected from adult male felons newly released on parole during August and September of 1970 (see Appendix for details of study design). The ex-offender interviewers conducted tape-recorded interviews, using a schedule containing both open-ended and structured questions. Ex-offenders and practitioners participated throughout the study in the selection of the questions to be used, in the interpretation of the results, and in making program recommendations.

The 60 tape-recorded interviews with the parolees yielded about 1,200 pages of transcribed manuscript. The respondents were selected at random from the total parolee population in San

Diego County, so, in that sense, they represent the "average" parolee, rather than selected spokesmen. Yet they have a remarkably skillful way of unfolding their stories, and they vividly describe their needs, the experience of being released from prison, memories of their time while in prison, and why they think they committed their crimes.

Of the 60 interviews, 14 have been selected, edited and presented in this chapter. These vignettes are not intended to represent in all details the rest of the parolee population, but they serve to bring to light most of the needs, experiences and characteristics common to the others who were interviewed. In other chapters, data from the 60 interviews are combined and presented, including findings from the content analysis of the transcribed interviews as well as the results of the structured questions and scales. By including portions of the interviews themselves, as in this chapter, the reader is expected to get to know the parolees, not so much as convicts but as individuals, each uniquely characterized by his combination of attributes, needs and experiences, and the ability to recount his story.

The parolees vary considerably in individual characteristics. They ranged in age from twenty to over sixty. Black, brown and white men are included. They have spent anywhere from 2 to 50 years in prison for crimes against property, such as robbery and forgery; crimes against the person, such as rape and murder; or for narcotics sales or possession.

The 14 transcribed interviews presented were distilled—a task of selection, condensation, rearrangement and focusing. The objective of the editing, however, was to be completely faithful to the full material and yet be brief. The interviewer's questions are omitted from the vignettes, and preceding them are capsules of additional information about each parolee. After the edited versions were completed, the material was presented to those whose "profiles" are drawn. They have confirmed the fact that the interviews are true to their views and statements, and have given us their permission to use them. The parolee's name on each interview is fictitious, as are most of the other names or places to which he refers. Every attempt was made to conceal the identity of the respondent in order to protect his privacy.

One year after these interviews took place, the parole agency records were consulted to determine what had happened to the parolees. That information is presented at the close of each vignette.

## I Never Did Expect To Get Out

Melvin Kost is white, 68 years of age and divorced. He has served over 40 years in prison—a notorious criminal. His crimes include kidnapping, assault to commit murder, robbery, burglary, and grand theft.

He lived with his parents during his early childhood and his father was a carpenter. Melvin began serving time in penal institutions when he was 13 years of age. He had been on parole less than 2 years when interviewed.

I've been in and out of the joint 7 times over the past 50 years. I went in at 13 and got out at 14, and I went in at 16 and got out at 17. Then I went in at 19 and got out at 24 or 25; then I went back at 26 and got out at 39. And then I went in at 44 and got out—it was 16 years—I got out when I was 60. I went back at 63 and got out at 65. I served 43 years altogether, and I've been on parole 17 months this time.

See, I grew up in a reformatory. I was 13 when I went in there and been in damn near ever since, except for 5½ years from '43 to '49 when I was in the manufacturing business. I made a lot of money then. Truthfully, I never did expect to get out this last time, by reason of the fact that I had all these life sentences. I was on the bottom and I didn't think I'd ever be free again. And I hardly think that I would have if it hadn't been for having a heart attack and emphysema.

When I did get out this time I didn't have any trouble because I brought $240 out with me, and before that was used up I was put on the Blind Aid—$190 a month (partially blind). So actually I haven't had any difficulty gettin' along. The first experience I had when I got out was in meeting some friends that I had left here in 1966, and I stayed all night with one of 'em the first night. He and his wife are real good friends of mine. Then the next night, I met a friend that I'd known at Folsom, and he found this boarding house for me. The first experience I had with people that I hadn't known before was with my landlady, and she turned out to be a real friendly soul that's been a friend ever since.

I'm a lot happier than I expected to ever be, because of my present location and having a workshop, a place to keep myself occupied. When I lost my eyesight, I had to learn to make something, and I remembered these turtles they used to have in a gift shop at home, so I decided to try to make those with animated heads and tails. And I carve monkeys. I used to make trapeze monkeys and dancing monkeys. I haven't accomplished a great deal though, except just to live good and be happy, which is the main thing. If I have any complaints, I would say my sexual life is a little below average. But at my age it's got to be, and I can do without it. I have done without for so long it's not a problem any more, but I still wouldn't mind getting married, you know.

What has helped me on parole was being able to find a place like this boarding house, at such reasonable rates. If they'd had a parole program something like the present-day program, you know, helped you over the rough spots, I don't think I'd have fucked up like I did. The friendliness of the officials in Vacaville sort of altered my opinion toward authority. One doctor was real nice to me, and whether that had anything to do with my attitude on parole or not . . . it did make me less bitter than I would have been otherwise.

See, when I came out of the Texas joint, it was the height of the '24 depression. And I mean it was tough! When I got out again in '32, it was even tougher because that was in the middle of the *big* depression, and it was a case of "steal or go hungry," and steal is just exactly what I did, too. Yet I came out with my mind made up to try to make it that time. I even walked 14 miles, 7 miles out and 7 miles back, to try to get a job digging ditches for 20¢ an hour. I would have made it that time if I'd just had a little bit of help. I had life then for killing a policeman in Oklahoma City, and I hadn't killed him either, strange as that sounds. You probably never did hear anybody holler "bum beef," did you? I didn't kill him, but I got life for it anyhow.

I did 6½ years then and I came out and said, I'll never go back, never go back. Well, hell, I did . . . been back ever since. That was in '24. In '32, I got out though, and if they'd had any sort of program at all . . . but they just turned you loose, with $5, and they'd take you to town. And the next time I got out, I had $30,000, believe it or not. It attracted national attention about me making

$30,000 in prison. I had the gift shop and, well, I made it every way that I could—gamblin' and financin' and . . . Yeah, I came out with $30,000. After I got out, I went in the leather goods business in Phoenix. Now there I had a chance to help ex-cons and I did, too, because I gave every one of 'em a job that wanted it. I helped 'em out by givin' 'em jobs, because of the difficulty I had during the first several times that I got out, knowing how tough it was.

It was rough in those days—like damn near fifty years ago. They'd handcuff you and tie ropes around your thumbs and tie you up. That kind of treatment just embitters a person. And it doesn't take as much money to help a person before he goes back as it does to keep him after he goes back, by a damn sight.

I think I've had some good ideas about what to do. In 1961 I drew up this plan for a home for ex-cons to come out to, and it would house 96. It had a workshop in there, and I wanted to be an instructor in this workshop. That was my primary reason for submitting this. It was to be about 20 miles out of Sacramento, and would require 4 or 5 acres, say, for a truck farm and one thing and another, so they could raise their own vegetables. I submitted it and I got a letter from the assistant director complimenting me on it, but they never did do anything about it.

And then these halfway houses came out along the same principle, exactly the same principle as I'd advocated myself, so I sort of feel that I'm the daddy of the halfway houses, because I'd never heard of it before, and I hesitated a long time about even submitting a proposition like that because it sounded so silly and so unacceptable to the public, you know. But they have accepted it now and it's worked. And in my estimation, that's the greatest thing that ever happened, to give a parolee a place to stay and security for the first few weeks or a month that he's out.

But at my age, for myself, I can't see a lot of future. I'll go along just about like I'm goin'. Fact of the matter, I'm content and don't have any aspirations I can't satisfy. I've seldom made any plans anyway except escape plans, and they generally turned out as I expected. I escaped 17 times in the last 50 years. I tried it three times in Folsom, but I didn't make it. I fell off the hospital and broke my tailbone and sprained both ankles once. That's one that didn't turn out! As a matter of fact, three didn't turn out right.

I'm goin' to make it this time by continuin' as I am right now. I don't have any desire for money like I used to have. Fact of the matter, I've had real easy chances to make some extra money but I didn't take advantage of it. I'm not going to take advantage of it as long as there's any chance of returning.

I haven't altered my attitude toward making a dishonest dollar, as far as the moral considerations are concerned, but I haven't taken a chance on doin' anything on the spur of the moment like I used to. I don't claim to have altered my opinion as to the right and wrong of it, though. All my life I've been hustling, and I'd hate to admit that I was a damn fool all of my life. The only thing is that the rest of my life I'm goin' to be content with what I've got, whereas I never have been before.

*Melvin was still succeeding on parole one year after this interview.*

## *New And Beautiful*

Leonard Montgomery is a black male, 35 years of age. He served over 13 years without parole in California state prisons on charges of theft and rape.

Leonard was reared by his mother and attended high school through the second year. He is happily married now, and has children. Though he was employed for a while after his release, he was laid off and has not been able to find new work; so he is receiving welfare assistance. He had been on parole for about six months when interviewed.

The first days out were just great, really, because I had been away for 13 years and to get out and be able to walk around was great. Even after 6½ months, I'm still sort of gung ho. I'll be standing, just enjoying being out in the streets, being able to look up in the air, or at the stars or watching the planes go by. I hadn't been able to do this for a long time.

People who haven't been locked up can't understand what I see in it because it's a thing they take for granted. You know, it's there all the time, it hasn't been taken away from them. It's a gas, bein' out, and I enjoy it and I intend on stayin' out.

It was a lot for me to get used to. It was almost like the first few days in the penitentiary, but not quite that bad. I don't mean it was bad bein' out—it was beautiful—but you know how you feel when you're new to somethin'. It's almost like being reborn. There are things you have to learn all over again, and things you have to learn. There was a lot of time between '56 and '70, and everything here was new to me, really, it was all new. New and beautiful.

My wife divorced me about two years after I got busted. But all the time I was locked up, I kept in touch with the kids, and then when I got a date and went to Chino—I had a 90-day pass. I think this is a terrific idea. I came home and looked for a job, and I got back and talked with my family. And me and my wife found out that although there are things there that had been smothered, they were still there. We decided to give it another try, and it's working out beautiful.

Now this was strictly between my wife and I. As a matter of fact, in counseling they told me they didn't think it would be wise for me to get married again. I'm glad to say that they were wrong.

I guess the biggest satisfaction I've got since I've been out is helpin' to see that my wife goes to college. She's been wantin' to do it for years and years, and she's never been able to do it. But after I came home, now she's able to do this. She says that I've given her the drive. She's always wanted to do this, but she's never had anybody to give her any incentive or make her feel like she could complete this course once she entered. I feel that I've helped her to be more sure of herself and have more faith in herself, you know. And I really believe that she's going to come out on top.

Oh, I don't know, there's so much, man. I just love it all. I love it all, and I intend for it to stay like it is.

Before I got out, I wondered whether or not I could make it, you know. I always felt before I got out that if I got out, I would be able to make it. But then after I got out, I guess I was a little hesitant at being really sure. The joint didn't give me any help, but my family did.

Well, after I first got out I explained to my family that it was going to take time for me to adjust to them and for them to adjust to me. I gave them a small rundown on my little moods and the personality I have. This is just something that happens after you do so much time. I'm gonna have to take time to get rid of it. And they understand, and we get along. At times I'm awfully quick-tempered, not that I'm violent, but I'll say something that's unpleasant. But this is not really me, and they understand. _

In prison I learned a lot about myself. I was an umpire, and we had to learn to cope with different types of personalities. It also helped me to be patient and try to understand other people and the way they feel. I really got somethin' out of it. I did my first five years in San Quentin where you stay your distance and you didn't associate. When I went to CMC (California Men's Colony) it was altogether different because it was under this UCLA program, with better relations between the inmates and custodial officers. I went there and I got off the bus, and I seen these inmates talking to the officers. It kind of threw me back a little, you know, because the first thing that run in my mind was "a snitch." When I came down to the ball field, I see this guy with these khaki pants on and a T-shirt, and I think, "What is this?" Come to find out, he's an officer. I wasn't used to this and it threw me a little. There's less tension in CMC than there is in Quentin or Soledad.

Like, for example, in Quentin the whites are white and they live by themselves, and the blacks are black, and the chicanos are chicanos, and they're all in these little groups and there's not that much mixing socially. There are smaller groups at CMC and the majority of people mix. And I think you can attribute some of this to the custody officers because I definitely believe that they cause a lot of tension in the penitentiaries.

I feel that a lot of things that happen in those places could be avoided if the officers would make the right decisions, and they know which decisions to make. They know, but they don't want to make the right decisions. As long as there's trouble or chaos or uproar in the penitentiary, they're satisfied, because this is their job. Let's be truthful about it, we have sadists in all fields, and I know that there is quite a few of them in the Department of Corrections.

Naturally there was times when I felt an officer was prejudiced toward me, sometimes because of my color, sometimes because of me as a person. As far as brutality, this has never happened to me, but I've seen it happen to other people, you know.

Like the first stabbin' or the first killin' that I saw in the penitentiary, you know, I felt that had there been a better way of handling the situation, it wouldn't have occurred. It happened to be an Indian and a black brother. They had had words the night before, and one white guy wanted 'em to be quiet, and so they made an appointment saying, "I'll see you in the morning in the chow line." Everybody in the block heard this, and I can't understand why the officer didn't hear it. You could tell just from the talk that he should have investigated it and did something about it, but nothing was did.

The next morning the brother walked right up there in line, waiting to get his stuff, so the Indian guy came up and started tussling. The officer run over and grabbed the brother and pinned his arms to his side. When he do this, the Indian guy go in his belt and come out with a knife, you see, and he sticks the brother while the officer's holding him. Nobody held the Indian guy, you know, they grabbed the brother.

This always happens, whenever two people are fighting. If there are two different races, for some reason or other, they always grab the blacks. I'm not sayin' this because I'm black, I'm sayin' this because this is the way it is. If there's shootin' in the yard, the first person they shoot is a black man.

So he grabbed the brother, and the Indian stabs him and kills him right there, right on the spot. And when they ask the guard about it, they have a kangaroo investigation, he said, "Well, I didn't know the guy had a knife." And, you know, they let him go. But the thing was if he was going to do anything, he should have stepped between both of them and pushed them both back, instead of grabbing one and pinning his arms to his side.

If I were a guard, I'd try to understand the men, and know one thing for sure, that because they've committed a crime, it doesn't make them less a man. They're still men, and they have to be treated like men even though they're locked up. And this is the biggest thing, really. Because you're locked up, most of the correctional officers feel that you're not a man and they don't treat you like a man. They treat you as though you were a juvenile or a child, and when they say something, they want you to jump, regardless of which tone they say it in or anything else, you know.

A man's just not goin' to be talked to like a child if he's any kind

of man, without sayin' something. He actually has to say something in defense of his manhood, you know, if it's no more than,
"Hey, man, you can't talk to me like that." And once you say that,
the first thing they want to do is grab the pen and write up dis-
ciplinary reports on you, which can affect your whole life. I mean,
it could cost you two or three more years.

In 13 years, I think I got 7 of them. But in my opinion, they were
petty. Like when I was a cook, they said I had too many eggs one
time. I overslept one morning. I didn't get to my job on time, you
know, and things like this. The last one I got was for fightin'. I got
in a fight outside the clothing exchange, but that was the most
serious one of them all.

I was on a cane, and I had been laid up for about two weeks, so I
finally got up and went out to change my clothes. I was tired of
asking other people to do things for me. On my way to the window, I guess I must have bumped into this other inmate; he was
high, white, and loaded on barbiturates.

So when I got my clothes and I was comin' back, he just threw
his shoulder into mine. That provoked me, and I told him, "Hey,
man, what's happenin'?" and he said, "You son-of-a-bitch, you
bumped into me when you went to the window and you didn't say
'Excuse me'." So, like I say, this is where the umpire come into
play, because any other time, we'd have just gone into it right
then, but I tell him, "I'm sorry, man, I didn't know I bumped into
you."

I started back walking, and, you know, I heard the footsteps,
the scuffling, and I'm on the cane, you know, and there the dude
is, and the dude started to swing. So, I had the cane and the first
instinct is, you know, just put it on him with the cane, but I
dropped the cane, and we got into a fight. We rolled all out in the
street, you know. And again, this is where the place of the corrections officer come in.

I'm on top of this dude, and I hear, "Stop it! Stop it!" This big
officer grabs me, and I tell him, "Wait a minute, man." I didn't
want him to pull me up off the dude, I was holding him. I said,
"Wait a minute, you hold that dude. That son-of-a-bitch is gonna
kick me." And he was standing behind me, and he said, "I got
him." So I was getting it up, man, you know, and that's just what

the dude did, man. He tried to kick me, but I saw it coming and I got off to the side. But nobody even touched him until after he had kicked me.

Another thing, I tried not to lose track of what was going on outside, you know. I always watched the papers and watched TV and listened to the radio, and I think this helped me not to be too far back. I think the men could handle outside entertainment, too. I really do. You know, like in other things, there's a few bad ones in any crop that you have. But they could be weeded out, you know. I think if they would let more people come in and be in contact with inmates, then there would be a better understanding of the inmate. You see, most of the people out there don't have any idea of what it's like in prison, or what the inmate is like.

One thing I found out that really surprised me when I got out is the understanding that some of the employers and the people had. They are more willing today to give you help than what they used to be. It's not such a bad thing nowadays. I mean it's bad for the individual, but the world don't look on him as being some kind of animal because he's an ex-convict. They're understanding more and more that anybody can make a mistake.

I made my mistake, but I'm going to make it now. I'm going to make it with my family—with their understanding, love, and willingness to help.

*Leonard was discharged from parole during the year following this interview.*

## Pressure

Oscar Alcaron is 31 years of age and brown. He has served two terms in prison, something over five years. The last crime for which he was committed was burglary in the second degree, connected with drugs.

Oscar attended three years of high school and has no particular job skill. He is divorced and has three children. He was raised by his father who worked as a dishwasher most of his life. He is out of work and money, and he is trying not to use narcotics. He had been out of prison for three years when interviewed.

I've been out three years. I'm supposed to get a discharge in about a month. I done some county work camp time for citations for driving without a license and stuff like that. I been in the work camp twice in the last four months and I've been locked up about four times. The first few days out, I didn't want to go to the hypes, you know, I wanted to stay away from the hypes. I wanted to stay on the freeways. In other words, I knew where I was going. I knew where I was going to go. I wanted to find out what was happening. So right away, boom, I go back to the hypes. See? A guy gave me a gig right away. I've been using since the early fifties, off and on, off and on, off and on.

When you get out, you're trying to make a change. I mean you prepare yourself. You want to do so many things. You want to make up for the past, you know. And once you hit the streets, man, you want to make up for the past so bad, you know. And you want to show everybody that you can make it. And hell, this thing is piling on you, this is driving you.

You see a lot of people. They say, "Hey, man, you're lookin' good, lookin' healthy, be cool." So, yeah, so now I gotta get on the ball, I gotta stroll, I gotta look for a hustle, man, I gotta get some bread, I gotta be cool. So, in other words, it's a strain. Once you get out you got all this pressure on you. You got all these ideas on your shoulders, preying on your mind. You not only disappoint yourself and your family, but people that are watching you.

Stay on the straight and get away from all this trash, man. Yet you come out with a good head on your shoulders, man, and once you put it to use, you can accomplish a hell of a lot—but there's a gap there.

There is changes that I've seen since I've been out though, 'cause before you always come out and you know what's going on—you know what the rules are and everything which you got to go by, see. And the first time you fall, the first time you ask for help . . . you know you're going to fall, man, you know you're going right back to jail if anything comes up.

But, see, now it's a whole different story. Now you can look for help. Now you can go places and ask for help. Now there's different communication at the parole office than there was before in the old school. Now they say, "This time if you rank it, man, come to us. If you blow it, man, come to us and tell us what you did. If you're sick, don't run. Come to us." See what I mean?

But the guys that's still in this old school that you and I've seen, they're afraid. They know that once they do wrong, they're going to go to jail. And nobody wants to go to jail. See, now they've got a parole department to come down and run it down to the dude, you know. Where if you guys get ahold of a parolee before he talks to his PO, and run it down—"Look, man, if you're going to get strung out or you need some help, man, come to us and we can talk to the guy, you know, and it won't be so hard." It's not like the old times, it's so different—it's a new thing. You see what I mean?

And that's what's important right now, man. A lot of dudes have been asking me, "Hey, man, I just got out. The man's gonna be on my back. Man, what should I do?" And the only thing I can say is, "Go to the hospital, man, and see the guys up there, the ex-cons. Go up there and find out what's happening, man. They can help you, man. Don't start running right away, because you get an APB out on you, man, and you're back in jail before you start."

But you got too much pride when you come out. You got all that pride, and you don't want to be humble, but you come out with so much pride that you don't want to ask. You want to get in and do good, yet you can wind up back in the gutter, man.

I had my people to go to when I got out. I had some threads there. I just come home, took 'em off, and put on my other clothes, put me back in the groove again. What they're doing to you now, I think, is giving you $49. From that you've got to buy your ticket and your clothes, and you ain't gonna have much left there. So when you come down here you've only got a few dollars in your pocket . . . $20 or $30, and you don't know how long it's going to hold you, and then you want to see some people and you're dry or something, and there goes half of that. After that you start thinking, "Wow, man, I've got to get some bread." So you're all wound up, and pretty soon, there you are, man. I don't think that's fair, though, giving the con such a little money and telling him to make it.

My old lady cut me loose after I got out, man, because she said I was going back to the same thing again. She waited for me—that was the year I came out, you know. So I tried to get some good gigs and everything, and it took time and everything, and she was working—she had a gig, nursing. I felt . . . left out. I couldn't do anything.

I just started going around and trying to look out for an escape, you know, and trying to get it off my chest, get it off my shoulders. And one led to another and pretty soon I was back in the groove again, you know. Like, where can I score (buy dope)?

I think that I've lightened up a lot though on being stoned. Maybe it's the fear of going back to the prison or going to the county jail but, like, I know there's a place where I can go to a man for advice and for help or assistance. And this is what a lot of guys don't know.

I can't go back to hustling. I can't do that because there's so much involvement out there. I just can't afford it. Maybe it's fear once you go down, you're going to get involved one way or another. I'm not working now. My kids are helping me with a county training program they have. I'm going to need some kind of counseling, though.

My biggest shame since I've been out is to go back again and hit on people. You go back up—they say, "Well, we want to help you, so come back to us." So the whole thing is that—walking back in and tellin' 'em, "Well, here I am." Here I am *again,* you know.

What really would have helped me when I got out would be like a welcome home thing. Here are your regulars, you know, and they run it down. "Hey, here's what's happening, man." Just run the whole thing down to them. That would help. That, and—everybody's human—you want a broad and to party for a week or two.

*Within a few months of this interview, Oscar died of an overdose of narcotics.*

# I'm Free, I'm Here, I'm Doing Fine

Christopher McClure is white, 22 years of age, and when interviewed, he had just completed serving a two year term—his first—for possession of marijuana. He had been on parole for two months when interviewed.

He was raised in child care centers and boarding homes. He graduated from high school in prison.

Christopher is separated now, and has no children. He is employed as a welder's helper. He is pleased with his job and plans to stay on it for a while.

The first few days out were a flash. That's all I can say, man. There's cars and dogs and trees and people, you know, and you walk down the street and there's mailboxes and there's houses and screen doors. And it all comes back to you. Things that you'd wanted to do, places that you'd wanted to go, things you wanted to see. It's all there, and you try to get them all at once. That's one reason why a lot of people are going back, man, because they're trying to do everything at once. I'm still flashing. Sometimes I still think I'm back in the joint, man. I say, "Wow, where am I? I'm free. I'm here. I'm doing fine."

While I'm at work, man, doing something, I know what they're doing (in the joint). Just fuck it, I lived there, and that's just a waste of time.

While I was living in the joint, I didn't even dream about the streets any more. All my dreams were in the joint, man, and going to the show, and standing in the fucking chow line—everything you go to has got a line, you know.

See, before I was in the joint, I never used to leave the house 'till 11 o'clock at night. I'd get two, three hours of sleep. I was a wreck. I was a fuckin' street corner hanger before I got busted! There was a big cement slab behind the garage, and that was our hangout. We used to have our names all over this big garage and carved in the telephone pole—it was a trip. Fuckin' cops were always comin' down. We were always running from them and shakin' them up.

They tried to pull so many raids on us. But we were located where we could see down both alleys and down both the streets, you know. And if we even thought they were comin', man, we moved out—endin' up on rooftops, bushes, and everything. They cruised by and they wouldn't see anybody, and then heads popped up all over the building. (Laughs)

I don't do that now, 'cause a guy started runnin' things down to me. "What does a cop think when you're out at two o'clock in the morning in a hot rod, cruising down a side street? What's the first thing the cat's going to think? 'What the hell are they doing out at two o'clock in the morning driving down the side street, or what are they doing hanging out on the street corner'?"

Well, I had all kinds of ambitions when I was thinking about getting out. I wanted to be a player . . . I wanted to have a lot of money. I wanted to do a lot of things that I haven't done, but you get out here and it takes money. It takes money to do anything. And you really have to work fast. If you work fast, man, you just blow your life, as far as I'm concerned. They stopped me, man, for two years and two months. They slowed me down, they put the lead on my ass. Now, I take it slowly . . . that's where I made my mistake last time—I started running.

So now, I'm goin' to keep workin' and keep clean. I haven't even been stopped yet. I want to stay healthy, too. If you just drop one, the next day you're goin' to drop two, the next day you're goin' to drop three, and after that you don't give a shit anyway.

But money is the hang-up because you see that's what this society is based on—it's a fuckin' capitalistic type, you know. You got to work and slave your ass off to get anything. Then, once you work, you haven't got enough money to get it anyway. I'm startin' to get hungry and want things, you know. And it's going to take me a while, man, because I'm no millionaire.

Like I went down—I planned on buying myself all kinds of clothes—and I had about $60. I think I bought about six fucking pairs of underwear, six undershirts, pair of pants and a shirt. That was it, man. That was it. And it's hard to get around town if you don't have a car. Christ, you can spent $5 on the bus in a day. So, like, if your parole officer could have a helper-type thing, you know. If you need help, you just call the cat up. "I gotta go here, and I gotta check out a job. I gotta go find a house." You can get some sore feet walking up and down the streets.

I thought I'd get out and go back to my wife. Then I got to thinking that balling is nothing. It was just a physical attraction. I said, "Well, fuck it; I ain't goin' to do it." While I was in, most of my partners sold my wife dope and made a tramp of her.

I think your ole lady should be able to come and see you about twice a week, on a night-time basis, for the guys that are married. They could turn their bungalows into little pads. You can stay there a weekend, two weekends, a month. That way you could kinda get used to your family, if you have any kids. Because you're stuck away for two, three, four years, man, and people change. I think you should get to know them before you just step right out of the joint.

I'm not sorry for doing time, though, because as far as I'm concerned, it wasn't a waste. But, you know, if I wouldn't of went to the joint, I never would have finished my high school. I never would've had a trade, and I'd be either pulling armed robberies, shooting heroin, or beating people up for money—doing something, man. Because my partners—the guys I was running with when I was on the street—I see where they're at now, you know, and it's fuckin' obscene, man. Shooting smack, man, and just getting crazy.

And, see, I was the same as them. I was really egotistical when I was out then. Like, "I can smoke more weed, I can drink more wine." I'd probably be dead or somethin'. I tore my ego down when I was in there, you know. When somebody doesn't like the way I look, fuck them. Because I'm not living to please other people, just me.

*One year later, Christopher was discharged from parole.*

## Even A Convict's Got Pride

Lloyd Nieman is white and 36 years of age. He has served two separate terms for forgery, and had been on parole for a short time when interviewed. He is a professional musician and he feels that running with the bar crowd and drinking excessively was in large part responsible for his "overspending."

Lloyd was reared by his mother, who worked in a factory. His friends have usually been cons. He attended school through the 8th grade only, which he has regretted most of his life.

The first few days I was out were about the roughest days of this entire period. I've only been out a short time—five weeks—but the first three days was a hassle . . . no money, no transportation, no job, and no place to live. Now these things have a way of working themselves out in time, but you have to contact the right people, and sometimes it's hard to find the right people. I was lucky enough to make a contact with a fellow at the Service Center and he gave me enough money to tide me over out of a fund that they had. I'd say that I had a pretty rough time. I'd say the first week was rough. A lot of walking, a lot of walking . . . .

I was lucky that I had two friends here, too, that could help me. Nick gave me a place to stay, because I was out of money within four days. They give you $60, and out of that you got to buy your own clothes, and I couldn't just move in without paying something, so I gave him $25, you know, for room and board. He didn't want it, but I think there's a lot of guys getting out that don't particularly want charity. They like to pay their own way. Even a convict's got pride.

I'd met Nick four or five times, and he kind of gave me a little coming home party. There was several people there that we'd call "squares." But he explained the whole thing to them and they just kind of accepted me as a person. They didn't shy away from me because I was an ex-con. Everybody was very nice, very friendly. They didn't go out of their way to please but they were just comfortable, nice. I think that's a big thing, being able to be comfortable.

I put in several job applications when I first got out, and I went through the ex-con bit on the applications. In fact, I thought about going back to music, so I joined a musicians' union. I was hired and fired by a club in 20 minutes because I was an ex-con.

Job training is a farce, as far as the institutions are concerned. I was a musician, but they want you to have a manual trade, so they recommended silk screening, which is fine. I have no objection to silk screening, you know . . . I might as well learn something while I'm there. So they made a big thing out of this. They programmed me for silk screening. "You got to have this for the (Parole) Board," they say. Well this is all well and good, but all of a sudden, they have an opening at camp. Now they need me at camp. So they send me to camp and tell me, "This training isn't really necessary. You don't need it to go to the Board." They need bodies up at camp, so it's not a question of what's good for you, it's a question of what's good for the institution.

Now I'm at State College on the EOP (Equal Opportunities Program). Whoever thought I'd go to college at 36? My head's kind of all aswivel because I've been away from school for so long. I'm having a hard time studying, a very difficult time because of the problem of getting back with it. I've been away from it for so long a time that nothing seems to sink in. Well, I'm going after my B.A., and we'll work on an M.A. from there. But I want to make it through education. I really do.

Financially, I'm not too bad off. I've got enough money now for about another six weeks, and I hope to get a job to supplement that income. I have a few friends and, right now, things are pretty good.

When I was in the joint, I kind of thought I might have to go back to hanging paper (forgery). I thought, "I'm not going to get what I want. I'll probably go out and get a job. I don't want to go back to playing in the bars if I can get away from it because I think that's part of my problem." I have always put on a front. I have an 8th grade education and the institution should be proud of the fact that I am in college.

But if this (college) had not come to pass, I probably would have gone back to work in the bars and associate with the middle class crowd or the high-paid bracket crowd, and invariably, I would go to cashing checks to keep up this front, you know.

I didn't expect it to turn out as well as it has. It's getting better all the time. My major disappointment is trying to do too many things too fast and realizing that I can't. The time that you're locked up is gone, you know, and you want to do all the things you've missed. When you get out, you're three or four years behind, or whatever it happens to be, and you try to make these things up. It's a disappointment when you find out that you can't do it, that it's going to take you a while to catch up. You got to go slow.

I have mixed emotions. I'm happy to be out, but I have a thing about being my own man. I realize it is necessary, but I do resent a parole officer telling me what I can do and what I cannot do. I believe that every man is different, every case is different, and there can be no set policy.

I believe everything should be weighed and judged on the basis of what the man is capable of. I don't think employment's a privilege, I think employment is a right! I believe you have a right to work anywhere you want. You know, you have to put *yourself* to the test. They're keeping you a mental weakling.

*Lloyd didn't make it. Shortly after his interview, he jumped parole and left the state. A year later, he still had not been located.*

## How Long's It Been Since I Laughed?

Phillip Sampson is white and 33 years of age. He has served about 12 years in state prisons for armed robbery and a number of parole violations. He had been on parole this time for a year when interviewed.

I'm 33 years old. I was only 13 or 14 when I went inside the walls. I've been in about 15 years altogether, the last time for armed robbery. You don't really learn nothing inside there. I just learned to live with myself and people around me. Now when somebody leans on me a little bit, I don't right away just want to bust their jaw or their head—I walk away, which I never did five years ago. Somebody leaned on me then, I'd break their arm. So, I'd say I'd learned a mental tolerance about things that rile you. Not everybody can meet my standards. I've got to lean a little bit towards somebody else. (Laughter)

The first few days out were strange. It's the turnover from the discipline. All of a sudden you've stepped out of it. You don't have somebody tellin' you when to go to bed, when to get up, when you can do this, when you can't do that. It's just a relaxed feeling now.

I've been very fortunate. Got a real good parole officer, and the guy is giving me every consideration. He doesn't look down my shoulder, doesn't put no weight on me. Only thing he wants me to do is make it so he can use me for an example. I mean, I'm a two-time parole violator, and I had the remark made to me just the last Board meeting—"Two strikes, and you're out." "I'm going to make it," I said, and when I do, I'm gonna write him a letter and tell him.

Nobody's leaning on me, which is a good thing for a person in my position. I don't need anybody leanin' on me. I lean on myself now. I think that's one of the major factors behind me making this good parole is the fact they're not hassling me, you know . . . "You can't do this; you can't do that; keep your head this side; shine up, man." That's what they do.

When I was in the joint, I thought about how I've thrown away fifteen years, and nothing. Literally nothing. Then, would you believe that I saw an advertisement that just pulled me up? It was an old movie they were advertising, with this guy and a gal just walkin' down the beach, not out there partying, y'know, and jumpin' boogaloo. They were just walkin' down the beach, hand in hand, and they were laughin'. WHANG! It just hit me. I wanted something. You don't have to have a lot of money in your pocket if you've got an old lady that you dig, and you can laugh. "How long's it been since I laughed?" I asked myself. Man, it's going to be different now. It just gave me a lot of fuel for thought.

And I'm fortunate that I met up with my old lady, and I got a "boss" old lady, there ain't no down-the-middle about that. Things were rough for me, but you got somebody like that behind you, that makes it a lot easier. We're going to get married when we get ourselves together. In other words, "Don't push me about marriage." If that's what I want, that's what I'll have. It's not like you want to jump in and then jump out—not with a kid and everything. So, I'll take my time on it. I keep thinking back to that advertisement.

And I've got to the point where I don't have to impress people, and I can give less than a rat's rectum about anybody on the street. There's a few friends that we have, but I socialize very little with people, but I'm not beyond giving a hand to a guy who's down on his luck.

I'm goin' to school, and when I do get out of school, I'll have a Class I Operator's License. That means that I can handle anything that's got wheels on it or treads, and there's good money in it . . . damn good money. I reckon men that's got any kind of intelligence at all, figure he'll make $15,000, $20,000 a year.

I've got my old lady, I've got the baby. I'm pretty well set financially. I got some of the money I inherited from my dad. I'm able to just lay back, cool it. My old lady works, by preference. She makes $100, $150 a week, which is nice.

But when a guy first gets out they should know he needs finances. That's the biggest hurt comin' out. Sure you can go beg a dollar or two off your parole officer, that comes out of his pocket. If he ain't got it, you're hurt. Your parole people don't give a goddamn. They stick you off in some flea bag joint, and that's part of it . . . they've met their obligation to the parole board. "I got you a place to live." A guy living in a hotel, meals, he's downtown—that rotgut area. He's going to wander around them bars, he's going to get to drinking, he's going to run into a few other sorry suckers, and pretty soon, it's a big vicious circle. I've seen it happen. It's happened to me, and no doubt it will happen to people for a long time to come.

They're getting a little tougher now . . . they want you to have a job before you're out. Well, jobs are hard to get. There's people walking around here highly skilled, and they just aren't working.

If you're a convict, it's harder. They say, "Here's a guy who's been in the joint," and right away, they distrust you. Can't blame them . . . the stories that they hear. Just the same, you have to prove yourself to them. Right out front. You know you got caught and gone in, and you fall out there, and people want to see which way you're goin' to go before they make any kind of an opinion about you.

Like I went to work for a guy in his bar, and he walked right out the door and left me in there with all the money and the combination to the safe and everything else—thousands of dollars laying in the place. He came back the next day and it was all there, so that's one way people judge you, like that. That felt good to think that somebody trusted you.

A guy needs some kind of a solid program. They need better community relations with people that are willing to put ex-convicts to work, and that's what I want. I want to be able to have enough finances to get me through, even if it was a loan. Well, you understand I was going to walk into a job that was going to pay me $87.50 a week, and I'd arrange to pay back the loan, whatever

I borrowed, you know, if I got it, without hurting myself. And I'd want a decent place to live, and maybe a chance to get some transportation if the job was out of the way, because bus transportation's the lousiest in the world.

I'm going to make it this time, though. I've got the attitude in my mind. I've seen guys down there on the street. "Hey, you, baby, I've got a little thing going here . . . six to seven thousand. Like to have you in on it; we know you're good." But I won't do it.

*Phillip was still making it on parole a year after the interview.*

## Do It, Die, Or Go Back

Hal Davis was released from prison two months prior to this interview after serving a three-year sentence for forgery and robbery. He is living with his parents now and working part-time. Hal is white, single, and a high school graduate.

The prison experience had quite an influence upon Hal, and he feels he has grown up a lot. He is twenty-three and believes he is not likely to make the same mistakes again. He hopes to keep his kid brother from learning the hard way as he did.

The first few days out were unbelievable, because after three years and three months, I didn't have the count, I didn't have the hassle. I was my own man, I could do what I wanted to, and it took me about three days before I really snapped out of it.

When I came home, I went on my own, thinking I knew it all again a week after I got here. And I lived with this other dude for five weeks. You know, I'm amazed, but, boy, it was "by my ass." You know, we wasn't eatin' too good over there.

My dad asked me to come back and take some of these jobs off him because he had to have an operation on his leg and can't handle it. And he kinda set my head straight because I know if I would've stayed over there, I probably would've went right back in shit again, you know, because it was getting deep as far as not eating and having to pay that rent and not working. I tried running those alleys the first week or two I was out. I don't want to go back to it. If a man can work and can hold down a job, he's got something.

I think one of my biggest problems was no transportation and no immediate job. I was hassled because I couldn't find work without transportation, and I can't get transportation without work, so it was one of those things. I been working for my father, but it seems like every time you get your head above water, there's a bill, man, that'll take you back down.

I really thought that I would be hassled more than I am, though. I thought it would be a lot harder on parole than it really is. I've been able to stay away from old associates, to an extent. You know, I still associate with them, but I don't let them influence me like they used to. I'm beginning to meet new people, different people. My past they know of because I tell them about it. It's really surprised me that my past has not jeopardized our relationship or caused these people to shun me. In order to make it, I'm going to stay away from the people I used to run with and stay away from drugs as much as possible.

Drugs wasn't directly connected to what I did, but pot didn't help it none. I let it lead to other things because I wanted other things. But I don't believe drugs was my biggest hangup. I think my biggest hangup was I was a goddamned kid who thought he knew it all, wanted the change in his pocket, the clothes on his back, and that nice car to drive. And I couldn't get it by working because I was staying too loaded on those drugs. So I'd steal to get it.

See, I knew cons before I went in, and I still do, but they're making it, man, that's what's so beautiful about it. Most of them's working. The others I feel are really trying to find a job. It really blew my cap, 'cause, like, you'd be bullshitting each other in the penitentiary, but on the streets, like, it's life. You gotta do it, die, or go back. In the penitentiary I got to thinking, you can't front until you're ninety years old and die, you know. You gotta have some kind of future.

A steady job starting the day after I got out would have helped. Unemployment is what's killing everybody. If a man can't find a job, and I've seen them really hustle hard, then they're gonna go right to their same old hustling ways. Employment's tight right now. Why, I couldn't believe it when I come out 'cause I always been able to find a job.

What really would help a dude is to have a job and a place to go, or he ends up at the YMCA, and that's no place to go to make it. You're goin' down there, man, with fifty other convicts living in that hole, and all fifty of them just gettin' out and they're all hurting for bucks just like you, and it just takes two of you to get together, man, and you're right back in again. Because a dog is gonna associate with nothin' but dogs.

See, I figured I was smart enough to stop school at 11th grade. But I went in the Navy and I finally got my diploma out of the Navy, and when I went to the penitentiary, I took a few more classes but they didn't help me any. My vocabulary isn't what it should be. It's too hard to get out of those old habits, talking to 2500 dudes. I hope this interview helps somebody, man, because they need to change . . . they really, really need to change. It's like they talk all that rehabilitation shit, but it ain't no good if the dude don't want it first of all. I don't care what you try to shove down the throat. If he don't want it, he ain't gonna take it.

In the penitentiary I seen what they called rehabilitation groups, and it used to make me sick. I hated to go into a group of people where all they did was cry and they wanted something, but they didn't want to go get it, you know. They wanted it handed to them. And I just got sick and tired of sitting in a group listening to some kid cry, you know, because, like, we've all been through it. And it ain't gonna help you to sit and cry; you been cryin' all your life. You know, you just better change it.

Now I wish I had more education—I didn't get enough. I have a lot of ability that I'm not really using, and I don't read enough. You know, I don't know what it is, but it seems like the longer you stay in, the farther you get away from the streets. You just start losing touch with the streets. I have a lot of acquaintances that got 12, 13 years in the joint. I think of them and how I done a measly 3 years. I think of the problems I had and I can imagine the problems they're gonna have when they get out, you know. They've been off the streets a long time; probably don't got nobody on the street!

That's another thing. It really blew my kid brother's mind when I come home from the penitentiary. 'Cause, like, he was a lot younger, and he looked up to me, like, "I can do this and I can do that, and I can party, raise hell, steal, fight and fuck it." He thought he could do it. When I got out this time (he's the age I was when I went in), I've been trying to beat it in his head. "Kid, go ahead, party, fuck, fight, do what you want, but you're gonna pay for it if you don't use your head when you do it." It's hard to teach somebody from the knocks, man. You know from yourself, when you was a kid . . . you knew it all.

I didn't know that when I was 17. I always had a roof over my head and food in my belly. When you get out on your own, that roof over your head and food in your belly, boy, it's a bitch to keep it there. They don't realize, man, what that roof and that food is. And what home is, man.

Home is beautiful. Like, you know, I never dug what it was, and I really feel bad about the way I used to treat my parents. I've changed. Like this morning, I crawled out of the sack with some broad to call my mother to tell her, "Don't worry about me. I'm all right, you know, and I'll be home soon." So I came home about 8 o'clock. I'm my own man and I do what I want . . . however, I still think that I shouldn't worry her, and I know she worries.

There are so many problems, man, that the convict runs into out here. So many, you can't name them all. Every goddamn time I run into a brick wall, it's somethin' that really hassles me. I had a car wreck two days ago. I ain't got any insurance, man, which I should know better than to drive, but I got to drive to work, and you gotta work to get money to pay for insurance. Luckily it wasn't my fault. I don't even look for them to do anything for me. But I'm *scared* of what they might do to me.

The way I look at it, man, the four years they took from me, if I were to work for four years, and had all that money today, I wouldn't have to worry the rest of my life. Invest it, man, it'd kick back, you know. But, that's the way I look at it. Instead of stealing $2,000 a year, man, you might be able to make $9,000, you know. I'm gonna try this trip. Maybe it's a better one.

Freedom's beautiful, I know that. And, shit, they can't throw you in jail for not paying your bills. If you get so drove up that you can't pay them, as long as you don't steal, man, I don't think they really can do too much to you.

*One year after the interview, Hal was returned to prison for possessing a firearm, which is in violation of parole.*

## *Making It In A Strange Town*

Anthony Mendez is a four-time loser who, in the interviewer's words, "has been around the block more times than the local transit system." He is brown, 46 years of age, and has spent over 16 years in prison—the last time for possession of narcotics for sale.

Anthony was reared by his mother. His father worked as a tailor. Anthony graduated from high school while in prison. He says most of what he knows about hustling, he learned in the joint.

This is the first time he has lived in this area, and he does not know anyone. He is employed, however, and hopes to meet people that way, because he is lonely. He had been out of prison about three months when he was interviewed.

I was just kinda lost when I got out. If you've been in a while, so many things are new and different. Your clothes are the first thing you have to take care of, you know, and where you're going to stay, your job, and how to get there—those things.

My family was my best experience. I have reestablished my family relations, but they live in L.A., and I'm in San Diego. They had a car for me, and they had saved some of my clothes which were six, seven years old. They gave me a very warm reception, and helped me with money and everything.

The first few days you just seem to be running around from one office to the other, getting things done. I've always been fortunate in this respect. I've always gotten a lot of help, so I think I've just been lucky; but I know there's a lot of other guys that didn't get the help I got. In fact, I've never even encountered a parole officer that was really what I'd call lousy, except one.

I really couldn't talk to anybody, which was hard. You get out here and people have their own life; they have their own things they have to do, and a lot of them, even your own relatives, they're in their own little rat race, so to speak, and they're involved in their things. And you come out almost like with your jaw hanging open.

I don't think the institutions as they now exist could prepare you to cope with society as it is today out here in the street. It's the institution itself that kinda closes your mind. It narrows your view, and when you come out you're really not prepared emotionally. You're seeking, and you're really hungry for some companionship, and it's hard.

It's an institutional pattern for a lot of people that when you are doing time you really don't get close to a lot of people; you're emotionally starved. You're very fortunate if you meet a friend that you can really go for, you know, a guy, a nice friendship, you're very fortunate. But for the majority of the fellows in the joint, they're so starved emotionally and so closed in, so shut off from any warmth, any friendship, that it takes a long time when you get out to break out of these bonds and be a normal person out here where you can talk to people and associate and socialize.

The institution is such an impersonalized thing as it is now. I hate to use the word brutalizing, but it shuts you up where you're all by yourself. You haven't got any broadening outlook on anything. You're closed. You haven't got anything, and you need something. You shut yourself off to protect yourself from somebody else's troubles because you don't want to be affected by 'em.

About the best thing that I ever really heard about was breaking down institutions that hold 5,000, 4,000 or 3,000 men. If a man has to be incarcerated, then he should be incarcerated in smaller groups that are regulated by age groups or intelligence, whatever.

Emotionally, the joint did nothing for me, I guess. As far as my trade's concerned, I have to say that I was fortunate that I did bump into some people there who took an interest in me. One guy has known me since the early '40s when I first got involved with the institution, and he got me down here so I could visit with my son.

But never did any official of the institution refer me to these people. In fact, they didn't want to contact each other. There was no information flowing back from one agency to the other agency which was actually supposed to be doing the same thing—help an inmate. I got this information from another inmate that had returned, and he told me, "Look, go to see these people." He gave me the address and the name and how to contact them.

I think that when a guy first gets out, it's a very important thing that that man go to work, if for no other reason than that eight hours is going to be occupied—it's going to keep him busy—and it's not going to let him dwell on how much he's missed and how much he's missing again.

Lucky for me, I kinda prepared myself a few years back by learning a trade, and I had that to fall back on. I knew there would be a long period here when I won't know anybody that's close to me that's friendly-like. Coming here is a very hard thing, but I think in my particular case it's essential that I go through this.

I figure it'll take me—particularly for my age—it will take me another six months, maybe even a year, before I'm on my feet and have established some friendships which will be helpful to me. I'm disappointed that I haven't bumped into a real pretty girl that just dug me.

Everything's going fine, other than that. I'd say I was in almost the same position that I was before I got into trouble, and before I came to the causes that got me into trouble. I think it's a feather in my hat that I am capable of making it in a strange town.

I'm working and watching my finances now, but I'm going to reach a point where I'm going to step a little better, and that's what I want to do. I'm pretty careful how often I use my car so I'll have it available to go to work. It's an old car and I have to keep fixing it. I just want to get up there where I can get some of this load off my back and start enjoying a little bit. I just have to hang tough for a little while. I'm in a strange town and I don't know anybody. I've been here only three months. How long can a guy be a stranger, you know, continually be a stranger? I haven't met anybody here. I guess by anybody I mean mainly female companions, and it gets kinda lonesome down here. That word is very seldom used in connection with a man or among men, but it's a very important thing. You do get lonesome.

I'm going to make it by working. I'm going to stay down here in San Diego until I have some clothes, until I have a good automobile where I can travel, and I intend to go back to Northern California where I know more people . . . unless I'm fortunate enough in meeting some big, fine broad that digs me down here.

I guess I'm basically a product of institutional environment, and I'm prone to look closely at a nice flowing racket, and if possible, to move. I think I got my outlook on rackets and hustling from the penitentiary when I was 18 years old—at that time they didn't have the programs and services they have today. You went directly to San Quentin. Then, if you were fortunate, you went someplace else. But that was my experience, and because of my later failures, I did go back, and I've been back, so that was my environment. So, my outlook is that I think I would "go" if I had some nice, safe hustle that wouldn't get me into a penitentiary.

*A year later, Anthony was still on parole but had lost his job.*

## I'd Rather Die Than Go Back

Jamey McDonald is white, divorced and 30 years of age. He has spent ten years in prison, the last time for forgery. This is the first time he has lived in San Diego, but he wanted to take his parole here, so he would be away from the people he's known in the past—"gangsters and everything like that."

Jamey went through the 10th grade of school. He was reared by his grandfather. When the interviewer asked him about his father, he said, "I haven't seen him in 15 years. In fact, when I was in San Quentin, the FBI was looking for him." Jamey had been out a little less than two months when interviewed.

I ended up in the joint because I wanted to keep up with the Joneses. All my life ... I'm only 30 years old, been in since I've been 18. I started off with the Georgia chain gang. I ran away with a girl to get married, and we stopped at a motel. Now this may sound funny, but I didn't have no thought of stealing. I went down to get a coke and when I came back my wife said to me (we'd only been married a few hours), "When we get home to Philadelphia, we won't have no television in the apartment. If we take this, they won't even know it."

I *did* take it, you know. I'm not going to say she *made* me take it, but I *did* take it, and I ended up getting three years for that. I knew it was wrong, but when I pulled in to the motel, the sign said, "Free TV." I told the judge this and he laughed; then he sentenced me to three years.

What can I say—I've been in all my life—all my adult life, I guess. I'm scared right now, scared to death that if I ever went back, I don't know what I'd do, 'cause I know how it is! Every time you go back it's worse. Like this time here—over three years straight. I thought it'd never end, 'cause I'd never been in a place like San Quentin. I'm not a scared baby, but I'm not a violent person either, and it upsets me pretty bad. I've done pretty hard time.

I've got a little nervous condition now, I guess, the violence in the joint contributed to it. I never had a nervous condition before, but I have it now. I get scared to death sometimes when I think about going back. You know how it is—informers, rats, and so on. I'm not that . . . never am.

There's mistaken identities, though, like in San Quentin. The year and a half I was there, there was something like twelve people killed, and four of them were people that was mistaken identity. And there are racial tensions. Like, if a colored person gets killed, they want to get even, so they'll kill a white, it doesn't matter who. It's pretty hard to settle down and do any time. I used to read a book a day, but every time somebody got killed, I couldn't read no more for two or three weeks, 'cause you think, "Gee . . . I mean if it was a racial killing or something like that!"

I wanted to go to school there. As you know . . . you can hear on the tape that my English is very bad. And I tried to go to school in San Quentin, but it was too full, they wouldn't take me. I tried to have dental work done there, and they rushed me through. They did give me half-way decent dental work—half-way. I'm here with half my teeth in and half my teeth out.

I was scared in prison. I always said I'd rather die than go back there. I just didn't know what it'd be like out here, though. You know, you dream all the time you're in there. "Jobs are easy to get. That's nothing. Just let me out and I'll get a job, a place to live." You really wanta work and make money and get a place to live. You know, you say this stuff when you're in there, but when it gets close to getting out, you think; then you are released and get on that bus, you start thinking it's not as easy as you thought it was when you were in there. Your main concern then was, "Gee, I wanta get out," and you'll promise the world to anybody. "I can get a job. I can do this, I can do that. I'm not like those other people. They can't work; I can work." But when you get out there, you're in the same shape as everybody else.

I was released from San Quentin into federal custody and they didn't give me any money, and I had no training in there or anything like that. Then when I was released from the federal custody, I was released with $50, and I was coming to a town where I didn't know anybody, didn't have anybody, no job or nothin' like that. It's pretty rough to get a place for $50. When I got into town late at night, the only room I could find was $7. When I paid my next week's rent, it left me pretty short.

I did get a job right away with the Episcopal services there. They only pay a few dollars a day. As soon as I'd get that together, I'd worry again because I'd have to get it together again. If you get a cheaper place in a run-down neighborhood, you run into all kinds of things you would try to keep away from ordinarily.

I tried for about four or five jobs, and I told all of them that I'd never been in jail, and it was one lie after another. You know how you have to cover up. "Where have you been for the past year, two years?" I was scared if I told 'em that I was in jail they wouldn't accept me.

A woman where I was applying for a job, after a half-hour interview, asked me if I'd ever been in jail, and I said, "Yes, I was an ex-convict." She stopped the interview right then and said, "That's it. I'll let you know." I never heard another word from her.

These people I'm working for have a lot of properties and a little money, and they're big-hearted people. This was a guest house but now they're changing it to a rooming house and I'm managing it. I feel like a housewife, but I want to stay out of the joint.

We put an ad in the paper, and I said, "What if any colored people come or Mexicans or someone like that?" And they told me, "It doesn't matter. People are people!" When I heard this remark, I decided to tell them I was an ex-convict, and I told them, and it seems like they're even helping me more now, so I'm doing very good there. They co-signed with me for $900 so I could get this car.

They're pretty decent people, but yet they have their doubts. Like the husband ... when he takes his pants off to change his work clothes here, he makes sure his wallet is out and is right with him. One time he forgot his wallet, and I said I'd get it, and he said, "No, no, I'll get it," real quick. And I wouldn't touch a dime of it. But people have their doubts.

I'm staying honest—I have no choice, because I sure want to make it.

*Within a year Jamey was returned to prison for failing to cooperate with the Parole office.*

## *I've Been A Thief All My Life*

Jonathan Henrik is 48, white, and single. He has only an 8th grade education, but has studied most of the time he has been in prison. He served five and a half years on his last term for robbery. In all, he has spent nearly 14 years in prison.

He is an electrician by trade and is living with relatives now and enjoying it. He feels sure he can make it by working and obeying the law and minding his own business. Jonathan had been out of prison six weeks when interviewed.

Ending up in the joint was just a freak accident for me. I done five years on a bum rap. I was not guilty of the charge. Now, I was guilty of a couple of things they coulda sent me to the penitentiary for, but the robbery that I was in the penitentiary for, I had nothin' to do with whatsoever. My car broke down and a guy picked me up. He had robbed a couple of banks, and I got picked up with him. The cop started chasing us for the wrong license plates. The guy had the red light on him, and he took off. We hit a tree and my head went through the windshield, and I woke up in jail with an indictment for robbing a store.

These people that identified me said I was one of them even though they couldn't pick me out of the line-up. There's people that knew me for 25 years, seen me in the jail, and didn't even know who I was with all those scars over my face. But these people identified me five months later. But you know how the police do that bit. A cop tells one of them chumps, "Well, he's already confessed. It's just a formality." What are they gonna do? They just walk in there and put their finger on 'em. But that was the only evidence in my case . . . just four people, all of them clerks in the store. Never been in the store to this day. Gonna go in it some time, though.

Loneliness, I think, is a bad thing for guys just coming out of prison, and you don't know any old ladies. I know a flock of them up north. They're all too old and decrepit to be driving down here, but I'll have to start correspondence with 'em anyway, or get out and meet a few around here. I really haven't tried to get out and meet any women or go honky-tonking. I'd like to find me some nice old widow woman though and live the rest of my life in peace and happiness.

Well, I really haven't accomplished too much. I gathered up personal tools and equipment to make myself employable, and I got me a car, got a few clothes together. When you walk out of the penitentiary with a little bit of money, it's not even enough really to buy decent toilet articles, much less do anything else. I'm telling you the truth—a man coming out of the penitentiary that doesn't have somebody to help him is in trouble!

If you haven't got no place to stay, you're going to steal something or do something. Heck, you just can't sit on the corner, can't get no welfare or nothin' like if you was some kind of minority member. That's one of the things that's always bugged me. These people all over the country are eligible for welfare and they work and everything, but they won't spend a nickel to help a convict. They'll spend thousands and thousands of dollars to keep 'em in the penitentiary, but the minute you go out the gate, they don't want to spend a nickel on you, and I don't understand that.

I've known some good men in the penitentiary, some good men, and I've known some of the worst in the world . . . the crummiest, lowest form of humanity. But there are some good people in the penitentiary—they're good for the world—productive, energetic, sociable, nice people, but due to certain different circumstances, they wound up in the penitentiary.

These California kids have some kind of thing against work. Every time you say something, they say, "Oh, you have to work?" So what? You gotta work everywhere. I don't understand their thing against work. I've been a thief all my life, I guess, and I worked almost every day in my whole life. Either in the penitentiary or on the streets or somewhere . . . I've worked every day.

Most of the problems in the joint is racial stuff. I never had nothin' against the colored people when I went in the penitentiary, but now I don't like 'em at all because of the way they run the penitentiary. They force these people on you, around you, and make you associate with 'em. Then they drive over everybody and they won't let you do nothin' about it, and it just made me hate them.

Now I've known dope fiends all my life and the only thing they do is spend all their lives in the penitentiary, and I don't think that's right. There's not one in 20,000 that ever stops. They know that for a fact. They know he's gonna keep right on using it, and when he does, he's got to spend most of his life in the penitentiary. Well, I just can't buy that. I don't like dope fiends. Never did like 'em because the dirty bastards will always turn you around for anything. But the thing is, I don't think they should have to spend the rest of their lives in the damned old penitentiary just because they want to shoot dope.

There are a lot of other people in the penitentiary that's in there under very dubious goddamned things that I can see. The officials don't even take the time to look or listen to your story or anything—it's really immaterial to them. There's only one thing that counts with them bastards . . . that's their job. What their little group is going to do on Saturday, how much raise they're gonna get, how much time they're gonna get off next month. I never heard one of 'em talk about a convict for no reason. Did you ever hear just two of 'em in a conversation? It don't have nothin' to do with the penitentiary, and damned sure don't have nothing to do with convicts. Feed them, give 'em clothes, give 'em their one show a week, and that's it. To hell with everything else. Everything else is immaterial.

It looks to me like they could all put out a little goddamned effort, you know, with all the bread . . . warden, superintendent, five associate superintendents, five program administrators, a captain, and there's so many lieutenants you couldn't believe it. I was there three years and I never seen all of them. There's lieutenants there that don't even know the warden. Now that's how the place runs. And the warden . . . I was there three years and maybe I seen him twice. I wouldn't have seen him then if I wasn't in his office fixing somethin'. He don't even bother to come down and see what's going on. This indifference! Shit. It's always rubbed me wrong.

I thought, "Well, goddamn, this is a penitentiary," but it's not. It's a big old social club for them assholes to run around there and play. You're there to take care of *their jobs.*

I've never thought until the last few years . . . if somebody hada told me that any person would deliberately keep a man in a penitentiary or the nuthouse or any place in confinement for their own benefit . . . but I've seen this happen in this state, and I know it's happening in the nut houses all over. That's common knowledge now, that they was keeping all kinds of people incarcerated, not for the good of society, but just for their own fuckin' job security. And you couldn't have whipped me and made me believe it. I'da called you a liar if you'da told me that five years ago.

I don't like the fuzz, and I don't believe in a lot of things they do, but there ain't nobody that low—but there is. And not only one, they all think thata way. "Hell with him (the inmate)," they say, "let's secure our position here. To hell with what happens to him. Give him another year . . . if he's a good man for this (job), why he can just stay here another year."

They don't do it outright, just to write up a bad report or somethin'. If you've been working, they just won't write up a *good* one. "I just won't recommend you for parole," you know. And it's just for the fact that they need you. I done a nickel (five years) on a first-time robbery and never had no beefs, perfect work reports all the time. I still did five when almost everyone else was gettin' out in two and a half or three. It was convenient for the employees of the State of California. It's beyond me, some of it.

When you get out, it's just as bad—prejudice—with people looking over their nose at you when they knowed you been in.

*Within a year of this interview, Jonathan Henrik had jumped parole and had not been located.*

## *Living By Principles*

Max Hutley is 59 years old and white. He has spent over 25 years in prison. His last sentence was for murder second; he had two prior felony convictions. Max had been on parole for 70 days when our interviewer spoke with him. He has associated with cons all his life. He lives in an extremely run-down hotel but claims he's getting along just fine.

I was in for murder second and habitual criminal. It was justifiable . . . I was pretty young, and the guy outweighed me by 80 or 100 pounds. He was a big dealer and he kept insultin' me, you know, and I kept telling the son-of-a-bitch . . . "The best you can do by foolin' with me is to get killed, man." And, goddamn, directly he knocked me about 40 feet, and I done . . . just what I did.

Everything has gone smooth since I got out. I wake up in a new world every morning, and things has changed so much . . . looking at all them little ole broads comin' down the street, you know, I'm just havin' a ball, you might say. Right now I couldn't ask to be gettin' along any better than what I'm gettin' along. Nobody bothers me. I just go, and I know I'm not able to work. I'm not raisin' myself on this phoney-ass disease I've got—emphysema. If I want to go to bed, I go to bed. If I want to get up and walk, I get up and walk, and I got nobody houndin' me all the time, you know. But I've got practically the same routine every day. You know, you're lost most of the time. I'll bet I make fifty trips out of this room a day . . . don't know where I'm goin'.

But I enjoy the eats 'cause I eat anywhere I want to. But you have no idea the money you spend just walking around with nothing to do. The cost of living beats any damn thing I ever seen. I know every time the sun rises, it costs me $7 or $8. When I go to bed at night, I say, "I'm not going to spend that much money any more," and you just can't keep from it, man. There ain't no way you can set down and eat any kind of meal without it costin' you more than a dollar. I eat chicken so damn much until I got ashamed of myself.

Your biggest trouble now is you get lonesome; you don't know anybody, and every time you try to get acquainted with a guy, all they want is to get you for some loot. I don't want to *buy* no damn friends. You know, it's the funniest damn thing I ever seen, it seems like you can't pick up friendships like you used to. Course,

I'm pretty much a loner anyway.

Friendship is what a person needs more than anything, though. I don't know if it affects everybody like it does me, but you walk up and down the street and all you're looking for is somebody out of the joint, you know. Well, you don't go a day without runnin' into somebody, you know, that's just out of the joint . . . especially if you do as long as I've done.

I've been around cons all my life. I was growed up in a small town and there was just three or four of us messed up. I was one of 'em. I had a half a dozen there that I thought a lot of and they thought a lot of me when I was younger, but, hell, they's all dead, I guess, by now. Only thing we done was shoot dice and play poker, steal watermelons, or things like that. Every once in a while we'd steal three or four old chickens and go out in the brush and cook 'em up, and then shoot dice the rest of the night.

I still have friends who are cons. They go by principles, you know. That's the main thing. I go by principles more than anything. I think that if a person hasn't got any principles, he ain't got nothin'.

When I was in, the fact is I didn't think I'd ever get out, to tell you the truth. I had trouble getting out of maximum security. You know, you couldn't get off that yard; hell, all you do is just play dominoes and shoot marbles. I was pretty healthy and finally got onto liftin' them weights. I think that's one of the best things they have in the damn prison. Maximum security knocked me out of all the programs they have. And then, too, when you're a habitual criminal like me, you're supposed to be lost anyway, so you don't get into rehabilitation programs.

When I got out, they checked me in that "nigger joint" and, hell, I didn't even stay all night.

I haven't had too damn many good things happen to tell you the truth. See, I've got a hell of a record, and I was always in the maximum security, enclosed—I've used the knife an awful lot of times in my life. So everywhere I was . . . before on parole, hell, they put you in jail every few days, man.

These parole officers here, boy, you couldn't ask for a better parole officer than what I've got. The only time I see him is when I go to talk to him. I think he's a swell guy, and after a man doin' as much time as I done, you can believe it's hard . . . a guy's got to be good if you're goin' to brag on him.

I haven't had no difficulty except that sickness (emphysema), and that's about the biggest thing I've run up against. I haven't had no beefs with nobody, no arguments or disagreements or anything . . . course I could have. I've avoided two or three of 'em . . . the guy'd be drunk or something, so I get away from him, that's all. 'Cause that's how I got in trouble before.

What I'd like to do now is to hang that parole up and go see if any of my people are alive, 'cause that'd been botherin' me for years. My father isn't alive, though, the old codger. If he'd of made his next birthday, he would've been a hundred. We was all pullin' for him, too.

*Max Hutley died of emphysema a short time after the interview.*

## Subjected To This World

Allen Lange is 29 years old, single, black and unemployed. He has completed high school. He came from a broken family and was reared by his godmother and cousin.

Allen spent 19 months in prison on a charge of burglary. He had been on parole for 21 months when interviewed. He is looking forward to a discharge and believes that he will eventually be educated in college and become, in his words, an "upstanding righteous citizen."

I guess I ended up in the joint because of my way of life, you know. I think the way of life is really a very influential thing, you know. Once a guy goes to the joint, this becomes his way of life. Everyone in my neighborhood were hustling, one way or another. This is their way of life. And these people who were neighbors were working on carwash jobs or menial jobs. They don't earn nothin' and that's why they have to get out and try to get somethin'. I know from my own experience. I started stealin' stuff before I even got in school. Even before elementary school, I was already stealin'. I'd go in a store with an empty bag and come out with it full.

If your neighborhood is bad, man, if everything you've got in your neighborhood isn't really for you, you're going to come up like I have in a world of crime, and that's going to be your life. As long as that neighborhood stays like it is, it's not gonna be anything but crime. And this is the type of word to use. I guess I was kind of wrong to say criminals, because in fact these are not really criminals. I don't really believe that they are. I believe they are just subjected to this world, that's all. That's the way they grew up . . . that's the only place that whitey will let him grow up at.

There's nothing wrong with hustling as far as I'm concerned. If you can make it hustling, make it hustling, as long as you're not hitting old ladies over the head or stickin' guns in their faces, it's all right. I'd rather go to school now though.

I would say probably the most vivid memories I would have of the joint would be of the violence that occurs on the inside. You kinda get close to a few persons because you almost have to; because it's one of those things . . . you have to have somebody watch your back because you never know when you'll make an enemy.

They didn't do anything to prepare me for parole. About the only thing they do for you to prepare you for parole is to make you straighten up in one form or another—attitude-wise. The board judges you for your crime that the courts may not find you guilty on. The court didn't find me guilty on it, but you have to plead guilty because of the police report downtown. I go to court for the crime and the people who are making the charges against me, they don't stand up in court. They don't stand up in court because they know they're wrong. I got busted sometime after my discharge date was up and, anyway, I pled not guilty to the beef before the parole board. The guy like to have jumped out of his seat, you know, and quickly give me a year denial. So, I go back the next year. So I say, "Okay, man, I'm guilty." They get what they want, so I got my release date.

They sent me to a halfway house. Financially, they didn't help me. I would have been all right if I had been situated financial-wise, with just a few clothes on my back and money in my pocket. You need to get around, you know. In other words, I had $15 and it lasted only a couple of days. People say, "Well, what did you do with the $15 you had the other day?" "Well, what do you think I did with the $15?"

It was mainly confusion when I got out. They preferred that I go somewhere besides San Diego because they figured this was where my sentence was and, you know, I agree with it to a certain extent but not to a great extent. But they gotta give me a better chance than that . . . my agent has to give me a little help if I'm goin' to make it in any city. They sent me to Los Angeles first. And I guess he didn't see things the way I see them.

I figure that anybody who has been incarcerated as many times as I have needs help. Yet, at the same time, I'm not really that much of a troublemaker. Not to the point where you could say I'm a menace to society or nothin' like that, but, of course, this isn't the way they look at it. Any time that you're busted, they receive a police report . . . and naturally a police report isn't going to lie! But my past experience with police reports in most cases is they lie as far as I'm concerned. They're supposed to be like the word of God or something.

What I see happening to myself now is using narcotics that I've used before . . . sort of puts your mind at ease, makes you forget your problems. Course I don't even have to get high to forget 'em. I don't have no habit or nothin' like that.

I really couldn't say if I'll be able to make it. I mean, like, I'm not goin' to do anything out of the way, you know. I'm not goin' to do anything wrong, you know. I don't know where or when I'm goin' to get a job. And like I say, I've got 14 more months of parole. That's a long time to just be walkin' around. I don't know why I think I can make it on parole just walkin' around on the street; I know it's gonna be too hard. It's gonna be just like last time.

*A year later Allen Lange was still on parole—nearly ready to be discharged.*

## Like Opening A Door In A Dream

Raymond Hinsel is white, 23 years of age. He served a one and a half year sentence in a California prison, a first offense for writing checks on insufficient funds. He says he never ran with cons or delinquents.

Raymond is divorced and has children. He is fairly self-confident and assured, but is concerned about his employment. He claims he doesn't expect a lot of money, etc., out of life. He made a single mistake and feels that he is paying for it beyond his incarceration. He had been on parole for one month when interviewed.

Well, when I got out, they gave me $42.50 and they said, "Okay, here you are, and there's the front gate." Now, if I hadn't had a family here in San Diego, and if I hadn't had the friends that I have, I would have been in real trouble. I might have been back by now. I mean I don't contemplate ever going back, but it could have happened.

Course I have a pretty good background before prison—a real good work record, and I've put five years in the service; I was wounded in Vietnam three times and I have three purple hearts. But generally everyone shies away from an ex-convict. They don't want to help.

As soon as you say, "Ex-convict," well, right away they say, "We don't have any openings." You can't say it's a prejudiced thing because they're not prejudiced, they're just scared. You know, the average person, they don't know what kind of person you are . . . they have no idea.

But I was arrested only one time in my lifetime. I didn't even know what the inside of a jail or the inside of a police car looked like. But I've got to pay for what everybody else in the past history of California has done coming out as an ex-convict; in other words, whether they've burned employers or whatever they've done. I'm paying for *their* reputation, not *my* reputation, because I haven't stolen from anybody. I've never taken a penny from anyone in my life. I've never assaulted anybody. I've never maliciously done anything to anyone's personal property. (He wrote bad checks.) But I've got to pay for what everybody else is doing by being an ex-convict.

I'm a little low on money now, but I know I'll go to work eventually. I don't need to be a millionaire. I've got a place to stay, and food and clothing, and I have a good parole officer.

But I think if you get past the first 30 or 60 days out, you get accustomed to being an individual again. You have to come out and you have to feel wanted. If you feel rejected, you're not going to make it, I don't care who they are. If you feel rejected by society, you're not going to make it. This is my feeling.

It's pretty tough, but if you've got any kind of will power and intestinal fortitude, you can make it. It's all up to the individual. There's help out there. I mean, there's small agencies, there's churches and things like this, that until you get on your feet will help you. I mean, they'll put out the extra effort. Like this agency here, they're taking all this information here from these interviews and something will come out of it. Might not be this year or next year or the year after, but anyway something will come out of it. And that's been happening, I guess, for the past four or five years.

It's good just becoming a citizen again...you know, just getting my feet on the ground, meeting people, getting in with the news. In other words, finding out what's been happening, what's new. So, just getting out and meeting the public, just getting to know people and to have them know me and to try to find some people to help me. And I think I've done a pretty good job of it.

I definitely think I'm going to make it. I told them before I left I would never be back. I'll never see another courtroom again. I'll never go back to jail again. I've had no confrontations with the law whatsoever since I've been out.

I feel that I'm an individual, and I believe in looking out for myself first. Now if I feel that I'm in an environment that is detrimental to me, I'm going to move away. And that's why I always stayed out of trouble. I never had any trouble as a juvenile, and I think if I could go that long, I can make it now.

*Within the year following the interview, Raymond had jumped parole.*

## *My Family's Been Carrying Me For 20 Years*

Ramon Jimenez is brown and 42 years of age. He has served 12 years in the "big yard." His last commitment was for petty theft, and he had been out on parole about six months when he was interviewed.

Ramon is a high school graduate, educated in the United States. He has two children. His most immediate concern is that he is only working part-time. He says he just wants what any guy wants—no more, no less. He figures he has reached the age of "backing off" crime and he is regaining some pride.

The first few days out were rough. The hang-up is contacts for jobs and the fact that I'm an ex-convict. I've looked as many places for a job as I've been home days. You know what kind of job those guys wanted to give me? $1.65 an hour. You know, a poop-butt job where you've got $46 if you work all week. I could make more money in camp. You dig what I mean? These are some of the hangups . . . .

They gave me a shirt to wear into camp. That's all I got. The dressups, you pay for. Well, they'll issue . . . I forget what the hell it is . . . $32, something to that effect. That includes that gunny sack they give you, and those paper pants and those cardboard shoes, you know, and they throw you out in the street and tell you to, "Go out and get yourself a job."

Now suppose I hadn't had a family. For a convict, the guy who wants to help himself, he gets turned loose, and what's he got? He's got $40, this burlap sack they give, and these old shoes where the arches fall after about six weeks. You know what the hotdogs look like in six weeks. And everybody in town, the minute they spot him, they know. It gives a guy a complex. Here the guy finally got out, and the guy may have good intentions and want to try to go straight, but how can he? You know, every time he looks this way, pow! Slap in the face, you know. Pow! Slap in the face this way.

See, I have no problems, really. Like, here, it costs me what? $110 a month. Then, like I say, this living situation (with a woman) here. Now they're beginning to accept it a little bit. The P.O.'ll (Parole Officer) come over, and he don't say too much. He'll frown a little bit, but he don't say too much. Where before,

"*No.* You can't."

Because over the period of years, they find out that how in the hell are you going to try and stop them if it's going to continue to go on . . . I mean, it's not breaking a law. The percentage in this town, or any town, or any big city, there are situations like this where people are living common law. Okay, now a convict or an ex-con almost has to. I'll give you an example.

I almost married one gal, but she got married when I was in the joint. So that was one out the window. So then I kept Maryellen, see, and I got pretty wired behind her, and I was going to marry her. So my parole officer tells me, "Well, bring her over to the office. I'd like to meet her."

So, anyway, I take her down there, and I'm going to go in the office and he said, "Wait a minute, sit outside." He goes inside with her; 45 minutes later she walks out of that office, and she was pale. Her eyes were "that big," and she's scared to death. And right then and there I knew. I said, "Well, this is one love that's adios. It's all over." So when I got her, I asked her what happened and she run it down. She said, "You know what? He told me all about your past." And I said, "So?" And I'd been living with her for nine months. Now this had never come up till she walked into that office and came out . . . and I knew. Well, I was telling her, little by little. But this is where the man kicks it to you.

So, now, like with this one here, from the word "Get," I told her everything! "You want to take me this way or forget it, you know. I'll treat you the way you would like to be treated, and all I expect in return is for you to accept me. That's all, and I'll bust my ass for you."

My family's been carrying me for 20 years. And they get a little tired of it and I don't blame them. I've exhausted them. You turn around and every time, you know, it's always, "Loan me twenty. Loan me fifty. I need a hundred." Like I say, if I ever get the opportunity, if these programs work out, you know, like you say, these interviews might help and it might do something in the legislature or whatever. I would like to reverse it, you know, and go to my family and say, "You know what? Here's fifty." I've borrowed 20 years from them.

But as far as me and heavy things, barbiturates, I mean, I don't tell her about it and then she'll ask me, "Did you? How much did you use? What did you do?" You have to do it like this. If you're going to be honest with somebody that you care for, you might as well just run it down.

Like you say in the joint, when a guy hits 40, or 35 even, he begins to back off. Not all of us, but a good percentage, and I think that percentage is enough to show the weaker percentage that they can make it also. And the younger ones ... God, it would have to help them considerably. You see what I mean, because they can say, "Here's a guy that's been in, he knows it and he's not jiving, and if he can do it and is making it, hell, I'm going to save myself 20. Why do 20 years like he did and learn it the hard way?"

Well, the parole officer took me down to see about a job the first night. I got a good parole officer. I mean, he doesn't bug me, doesn't bother me. I see him now and then, and the first time I got a ticket for driving without a license, I was shitting in my pants ... "That does it, Jeez, a violation." So I let it bug me for about a month. I didn't want to tell him. So finally one day he drives up and I just said, "You know what? I got a hassle." He said, "What's the matter?" I said, "I got a ticket for driving without a license." He said, "So? It's going to cost you 70 bucks."

Well, now, here ten or twelve years ago, you told a parole officer that, you know, he'd of said, "Well, come on down to the office." And, "Goodbye, Charlie." Or, a five or six weeks' sweat-out and then jail. But now that's changed.

In other words, he doesn't bother me, he doesn't bug me. In fact, I've got a bill from a local loan where I owed them some money ... I don't know, $500. I'm not going to talk to him about it because I don't think it's his affair. But he didn't forward my address to them. They wrote to me, care of him, and he sent me the letter. And I might take them to court on it because they took the car. Of course, I abandoned it ... when they're violating somebody to the pen, what else can you do? I can't take it with me, see? So they repossess it. And now they want *me* to pay *them.*

That was 1960. See what I mean? And the cusses want to charge me interest now for ten years. Well, that's cool, see, $278 plus ten years' interest. No way! Of course, it's the principal plus. Now I'm going to make a deal with them. If I get a good steady job, I'll pay them the principal, the $278, just to get them off my back, but the interest? I'll tell 'em, "You'll have to send me back to the tank. I ain't going to get you rich. You're a bunch of loan sharks. You got your car, you want me to pay you back, uh-unh." What can they do, put me in jail? They know they ain't going to scare me with no jail. I'm trying to handle the problem by paying them, but you can't pay them until you get a good steady job. So these are the little hangups.

But I'm doing okay. I'm not hungry, and I have a place to stay and I got a few threads. They're old-fashioned, made back in 1874, but they're threads. I'm not going to get wet, you know, in the rain. I got a little shot in the refrigerator, I got a little TV, I got, you know, these little essentials. But I want more than that. I want just like any working guy, that's all. I'm not asking for much. I'm just asking for a good steady job. Now where do you get 'em at?

I've accomplished a lot. I've accomplished the fact that my mind is stable, I'm sober, I can think, I can rationalize. I'm not up in the hall. In other words, I like it out here. It's beautiful. It's beautiful. Sometimes I go to the beach. It's beautiful out there. I jump in the ocean and act like a kid, you know, and roll around in the waves. It's beautiful. Can't do that in the big yard.

You see, I don't have to go in now and watch one of them old cowboy pictures that they show in the joint. You go back now, you'll see the same ones they showed twenty years ago and they're still showing them. But now I can go see the latest one.

So, this I've accomplished. In my own mind, I've accomplished a lot of things in this respect. I mean I've succeeded in accomplishing these things, and mainly . . . not using drugs of any form.

Now, that's an accomplishment after six months. I have no yen. I have my self-respect back. I have my family's respect and esteem, which is a hell of an accomplishment. You see, where before when I'd go visit, they'd hide everything, you know. "Lock up everything; here he comes." Now I can just walk in, no problem. I have my pride.

*A year later, Ramon is still on parole, with no violations.*

Chapter 2
# Theoretical Perspectives

Three theoretical explanations for the causes of crime are commonly used and by extension they are relevant to an understanding of recidivism (a return to crime after release from prison). Many of the ideas expressed by the parolees in this study reflect one or the other of these theories.

The first theory combines the notion of anomie and differential opportunity. It is a rather encompassing theory which asserts that while our society establishes goals for individuals, there exists a disjunction between those goals and the means which some people have to achieve them. This disparity may result in the use of illegitimate means to achieve the desired ends. Other individuals may simply use illegal means as the shortest, easiest way of reaching their goals, especially if there is a breakdown of social controls, for example, family disorganization. (This explanation combines the theories of Merton, 1938; Shaw, 1942; Turner, 1954; Merton, 1957; Cloward, 1959; Cohen, 1959; Meier and Bell, 1959; Cloward and Ohlin, 1960; Clinard, 1964.)

The relation between crime and the disparity between goals and means is discussed in detail in Chapter 5. The general trend seems to be that the ex-offenders are lacking in resources to achieve even an average living and ordinary kinds of life-satisfactions. Indirectly, some allude to the fact that their reach has, in the past, exceeded their grasp, and they intend to change that. You will recall from the previous vignettes that Melvin Kost (at age 68) said "The only thing is that the rest of my life I'm goin' to be content with what I've got, whereas I never have been before." Similarly, young Christopher McClure said he had "all kinds of ambitions" when he was thinking about getting out, "like having money," but now that he's out he realizes he is going to have to take it slowly. Ramon Jimenez (at 42 years of age) is ready to "back off crime and settle for what any working guy has." His difficulty is that he cannot get a full-time job, so he may need to lower his sights even more. Or as Lloyd Nieman indicated in his interview, he just aspires to "rise to a position of security and comfort legitimately and to have a wife, family, car, and house." He was going to college and working toward that goal at the time, but then he jumped parole, which may indicate that he couldn't wait for the legitimate means of achieving his goal. He had served his previous sentence for forgery.

A second general explanation, expanded in Chapter 6, comes from Sutherland's theory of differential association, which suggests that criminal behavior can be viewed as a subcultural phenomenon, in which deviant activities are learned or acquired from others. This perspective says that "a person becomes delinquent because of an excess of definitions favorable to violation of law over definitions unfavorable to violation of law" (Sutherland and Cressey, 1960). These definitions are most commonly obtained through association and interaction with significant others, e.g., family, friends (See Thrasher, 1927; Tannenbaum, 1938; Shaw, 1940; and Shaw and McKay, 1942; for their discussions of gang delinquency and association.)

Many of the 14 parolees whose stories you have just read speak of having been influenced by associates involved in crime. Those associations are referred to in three ways: First, and the one probably intended by Sutherland, is association with juvenile delinquents and criminals which occurred prior to going to prison. The second type of association, however, comes from the prison experience itself, and the third occurs upon release.

With regard to the first type of association, you will recall Jamey McDonald, whose neighborhood, friends and family all seemed to be involved in crime; the FBI was, in fact, looking for his father. Jonathan Henrik freely asserted that he had been a "thief all of his life." Christopher McClure (white and 22 years of age) said that most of his friends were cons and he goes on: "I was a fuckin' street corner hanger." An explanation is offered by Allen Lange, a black, who said, "If your neighborhood is bad, man . . .

you're going to come up in a world of crime." An interesting contrast to this was Raymond Hinsel, a young white man who said he was only arrested once in his life and he always stayed away from trouble. (He subsequently jumped parole, however, so his "association" with trouble is probably just beginning.)

With regard to the second type of association—the prison itself—two of the parolees in the previous vignettes say it best: Anthony Mendez, who spent 16 years in the joint, says he got his outlook on rackets and hustling from the pen, beginning when he was 18. Melvin Kost, who spent 40 years in prison, was asked if there was crime and delinquency where he grew up and he responded that he grew up in a reformatory and spent most of his life in prison, so that was all the life he really knew.

In the previous chapter the parolees also expressed concern about "bad associates" upon release from prison. Hal Davis, who spent a short time in prison, says that he is staying away from old associates, and not letting them influence him as they did before. But for others, most of the people they know are cons; for example, Max Hutley, who served 25 years said "You don't go a day without running into somebody you know that's just out of the joint." Actually, the theory of differential association underlies a portion of the "Conditions of Parole" in California, which prohibit ex-parolees from associating with former inmates of penal institutions and further prohibit parolees from associating with "individuals of bad reputation."

The third theoretical viewpoint, neither as widely discussed or formalized, is self-theory. The self-theory explanation, expanded in Chapter 7, includes aspects of the above two theories, but incorporates additionally and uniquely the idea that the individual's concept of self and situation, and the relationship between these two, affect individual acts. It involves status inconsistency, self-esteem, self-concept, and labeling. Labeling suggests that if the role of "offender" or "delinquent" is reinforced by others, the person will be more likely to see himself in that way, and his behavior will continue to reflect the offender role. Becker (1963: 31-34) says that one of the most crucial steps in a deviant career is the experience of being caught and labeled a deviant. This experience, he adds, has important consequences for the deviant's further social participation and self-image. Becker regards labeling a person as a type of self-fulfilling prophecy which contributes to his future actions and opionion of himself. Self-concept* is a complex set of attitudes, feelings, perceptions, and evaluations, learned through socialization processes in interpersonal and institutional settings, that the individual has concerning himself as a social object. While the individual occupies social positions and plays appropriate roles, he has experiences which he organizes into a conception of self and the place of that self in social relations, which in turn influence his choice of behaviors (McPartland & Cumming, 1958). In short, the self-concept has motivational and behavioral consequences.

The self-concept is of special importance when the prisoner is released because he has gone through a series of dehumanizing experiences during his incarceration, many of which you have read of in the previous chapter. Leonard Montgomery (black, 35 years of age) provides a fine example: "A man's just not goin' to be talked to like a child if he's any kind of man without sayin' something. He actually has to say something in defense of his manhood."

Leonard talks, above, about the struggle for self-esteem within the prison setting. Another parolee, on the other hand, suggests that his ego got him in trouble in the first place—"I was really egotistical when I was out then. Like, I can smoke more weed. I can drink more wine." Phillip Sampson had experienced this, too, but now views it somewhat differently because he said he was at a point where he just doesn't feel he has to impress people. Similarly, upon release from prison the importance of self-concept arises when Oscar Alcaron, a brown parolee, said: "But you got too much pride when you come out. You got all that pride, and you don't want to be humble . . . ." What will be discussed in detail in Chapter 7 is the pervasive finding that the parolees in general do not feel connected to the larger society. The consequences of this are suggested by Raymond Hinsel in his vignette when he states: "You have to come out and you have to feel wanted. If you feel rejected, you're not going to make it, I don't care who you are."

The theories just discussed are apparent in varying degrees throughout the cases of the parolees in this study. Keep these theories in mind when reading in the following chapters the results of the interviews with the 60 parolees, as we discuss what the parolee experiences when he is released from prison; what he perceives his most pressing needs to be; his levels of aspiration; his relations with others; and his relation to society. Consider what strategies can be developed to deal with the problems of the parolee because when they are not solved we face the good possibility of his returning to crime. The return to crime is of concern to everyone— to practitioners, to the offender himself, to the community in which he lives, and to society as a whole.

---

*This definition draws from those of: Kuhn, 1960; Kuhn & McPartland, 1954; McPartland, Cumming, & Garretson, 1961; Schmitt, 1966; and especially from Mead as presented in Strauss, 1964. For general works on the self, see: Gordon & Gergen, 1968; Manis & Meltzer, 1967; and Wylie, 1961.

Chapter 3
# Getting Out

## Who is on Parole?

- *60% of the parolees studied are between the ages of 18 and 35.*
- *15% are black, 22% are brown, and 61% are white.*
- *50% have not finished high school.*
- *72% are single, divorced, or separated.*
- *42% committed crimes against property; 27% committed crimes against persons; and 22% of the crimes committed involved narcotics.*
- *73% of the parolees getting out have served more than 3 years in prison.*
- *50% have served more than 5 years in prison.*
- *20% have served more than 10 years in prison.*
- *36% have served at least 2 terms.*
- *43% have previously been out and returned to prison.*

As of August, 1970, there were 592 adult male felons on parole in San Diego County. A sample of 30 parolees was randomly selected for interviewing (original sample). An additional sample of 30 was drawn from those who were released in August and September of 1970 (new parolee sample). The original sample and new parolee sample are similar in their identifying characteristics, and the combined sample closely resembles the total parolee population from which it was drawn. Therefore, inferences about the total population drawn from the sample are justified. In other words, the sample provided us with an accurate estimation of the characteristics of the total population. Where significant differences do occur between the total population and the sample or between the original sample and the new parolee sample, they are brought out in the discussion. The descriptions of the total population and the sample are shown on Tables 10 and 11 in the Appendix.

## What Parole Means

When a person commits a felonious crime and is charged and found guilty, he is given an indeterminate sentence—a sentence, for our purposes, which is served in the California State Prison system. He serves at least the minimum of the sentence and then he may be released from the penal institution on parole, on condition that he will maintain good behavior and remain under the custody and guidance of the state.

Parole has existed in some form in the United States since 1776, but the notion of *treating* or *guiding* the parolee is relatively new. Even now, the treatment on parole is minimal and guidance is limited, due in large part to excessive caseloads and inadequate financing. Parole in its present form was adopted into the law of 1869 in New York at the Elmira Reformatory (Sutherland & Cressey 1960: 568). The parole board, conditions for parole, eligibility for parole and so on, vary from state to state and between federal and state correctional systems, but in California they are basically as described below.

The California Adult Authority (CAA), as the general state parole board, is located outside the Department of Corrections and has authority to release from any state prison. The CAA has a full-time salaried board comprised of people in the field of corrections. Critics argue that the prison staffs know best who should be paroled, and they are the ones who should decide. This is the procedure in some states, but the CAA has proven comparatively effective in California (Sutherland & Cressey 1960:56). The inmate, some months before he is due to appear before the parole board, works with a counselor to devise a parole plan which usually must include promised employment. He may be "Released Upon an Approved Parole Plan" (RUAPP).

If the inmate's parole plan is approved and he is released, he will be given his conditions of parole, which may vary for different individuals. For example, some parolees will be forbidden to drink alcoholic beverages; no parolee is to drink to excess or use drugs which are not prescribed. The usual parole conditions are that a parolee may not marry, move, change jobs, engage in business, sign certain contracts, associate with former inmates, or travel out of the county without approval from his parole agent. Civil rights have been suspended by law upon conviction. When a person is discharged from parole, all political rights, except the right to vote, are restored. A parolee must file for a Certificate of Rehabilitation in order to receive a pardon and to have his voting rights restored. If a pardon is granted as a result of this, he can then register to vote, is eligible for public office and could obtain a professional license. The fact of the conviction still remains, however, and is taken into consideration by licensing authorities.

When the inmate is released he is assigned a parole agent in the community in which he will reside. He must check with his agent within the first few days of his release and must make a written report of activities to him once a month. A parole officer may excuse the requirements of visitation and the written report if he chooses.

The methods of supervision an agent uses will vary. Sutherland and Cressey (1960:573-574) say there are three varieties: watchdogging, inspection, and assistance. Police-work or watch-dogging is based on the belief that "parole is a system of lenience allowing early release of dangerous criminals." Inspection, on the other hand, is based on the assumption that reformation is a matter of individual self-determination, so the agent merely checks to see if the man is violating his parole. Assistance, reformation and guidance are based on the belief that adjustment has to occur after the offender is released from the institution. The type of supervision may vary within a given supervisory unit, and often supervision depends upon the type of crime committed by the parolee. A parole agent's caseload may vary from 35 to 90 parolees.

If a parolee violates his parole conditions, he may be returned to prison without trial, although there are hearings and the reasons for returning him to prison must be justified. If a parolee commits a new crime, he must be tried, sentenced (if found guilty) and returned to serve an additional term. The length of time a person is on parole will vary from state to state, but the average time is two years. It is now mandatory in California that each parolee's case be reviewed for his possible discharge after the first two years, and reviewed *each* year thereafter. Parole violations usually occur in the early months of the parole period, with the majority of infractions occurring within the first six months.

Usually there is a great deal of apprehension on the part of the prisoner, in anticipation of stringent parole rules. Glaser (1964:511) suggests that if prisoners are around too many returned parole violators, they will have unrealistic fears of their chances of receiving parole violations. Parole violation in itself is not as great a concern to practitioners as the problem of return to crime and to prison—recidivism.

Recidivism rates vary widely. Sutherland and Cressey, from their research, report that one-half of those incarcerated will go back to prison (Arnold 1965:212). More recent studies claim a rate of one-third. The present long-range goal of the California State Department of Corrections is to reduce recidivism to 25%.

## Stigma

The man who is freed from prison often carries with him the same problems which caused him to commit his crime. These conditions are now intensified by the stigma of his having been incarcerated, and consequently being labeled an ex-con.

> *I've got the work experience, but being an ex-con is putting the hang-up on me. They make it so hard for a person to make a decent living.*
>
> San Diego Parolee, 1970

With this stigma, a few dollars in his pocket, a ticket home (if he has a home), a job promised (which may not materialize), and some clothes, the released prisoner faces the world, nominally a free man. But he is also on parole, which means that he is under greater pressure to conform to traditional mores, customs and laws than is the average citizen, or he risks receiving a parole violation and being returned to prison. And, in fact, at least one out of three will return to prison. The man who is freed from prison knows these odds; many have experienced it themselves:

> *I knew getting out was going to be hard. It wasn't the*

*first time, and I said, "Goddamn, here's the same old shit
over and over again."*

San Diego Parolee, 1970

## Socialization Process

The parolees, in most cases, have not been rehabilitated; instead, prison has socialized them into a role which is of little use to them when they are released. Prisons are "total institutions" in that they have total control over the activities of the individuals within them. It has long been noted that such total institutions as prisons (Irwin, 1970) or mental hospitals (Goffman, 1961) are complex social systems with their own sets of defined roles, expectations and rigidly established patterns of interrelationships among people within them. Because of the specialized functions of such institutions, they must of necessity socialize their members into different roles and codes of conduct than those of the larger society. Inmates learn the convict code, the expected behavior toward authority, and how to relinquish power with regard to choice or decision-making involving the activities of their daily lives. In short, the inmate is socialized toward becoming a good member of the prison community. One prisoner said that "you're so used to being told what to do while you're in—'Button your shirt, put your collar down, tie your shoes, sit down, stand up, shut up, line up, lock up'—that you're kind of lost when you get out." Most students of this socialization process believe it handicaps rather than helps the inmate become a good member of the larger society. (For a general review of socialization as a process, see Goslin, 1969.)

Before getting out of prison, the parolee has had a prolonged exposure to this specialized socializing process. Of the 60 parolees, only 27% have served as little as one or two years, while 73% have served three or more years; 50% have served five or more years and 20% have served ten or more years!

It is important to keep in mind that many parolees have been in and out of prison before. The 60 parolees in our sample have had a total of 131 release experiences. Over one-third (36%) have served two or more terms and 43% have been released and returned to prison either on a second offense or for parole violation. Thus, 43% have experienced the full cycle of being freed from prison, returned to prison, and freed again.

## Rehabilitation Myth

As soon as a person is imprisoned, a program of rehabilitation for his return to society as a productive citizen is begun; treatment, however, is seen as a "bust" by convicts and administrators alike (Irwin, 1970:52). Short (1970:43) says that prisons in the United States have failed miserably in their much publicized aim of rehabilitating the criminal offender.

In this survey, in fact, when the 60 parolees were asked, "What did the joint from which you were released do to prepare you for your parole?" 70% at first responded, "Nothing," or "Not much." When the questioning was pursued, 36% of the total, who had first said "Nothing," later named something, while 30% immediately named something that the prison had done. The two items most frequently mentioned were job training and money. Some stretch of the imagination is needed to see $50 as effective help in launching an ex-convict back into a wary, if not actively hostile society.

For the most part, the parolees in this study felt neither helped nor rehabilitated as a result of their time in prison. Most clearly did not like their experience in "the joint" and declared that they never wanted to return, e.g., "I don't want to go back. I'm not going back, ever!" Most professionals in corrections would probably agree that it is a desirable effect when a person does not want to return to prison, but it has not been shown that a negative experience in prison, per se, serves as a deterrent to returning to crime.

Irwin (1970:58) says that inmates believe they receive cruel and unusual punishment. It is not likely that such a belief can have a positive effect on future attitudes or behavior of ex-cons.

> I've heard about prisons being bad all my life, but I thought people were exaggerating. I heard about going to visit them and how they'd mistreat women, but I thought, "Oh, come on, this is America, and these things don't happen."
> Parolee's girlfriend after visiting a jail, San Diego, 1970

Of the 21 parolees who evaluated their time in the joint, not one saw it as a positive experience and 71% saw it as clearly negative.

The examples most frequently given were expressions of fear, the fight for survival, violence, brutality and pressure. One of the more extreme examples follows:

> *Well, of course, we had the stabbings, the killings; prisoners were killing guards, guards were killing prisoners, prisoners were killing prisoners; they were having riots a lot.*
>
> San Diego Parolee, 1970

A common form of "correction" used within the prison walls is isolation. Such experiences usually leave a vivid impression on the inmate:

> *I was in maximum custody—very restricted—for three years. I was confined to a 200-square yard area, which gets very, very monotonous. You see the same blade of grass every day.*
>
> San Diego Parolee, 1970

Many parolees think that isolation can, in fact, be devastating to an inmate:

> *One Chicano guy was very creative as an artist and writer. But he was in isolation for 30 days in a little room, and I think that confinement was the cause of his suicide. We had suicides often.*
>
> San Diego Parolee, 1970

There is also the fear of sexual molestation and a general lack of feeling of security within the prison walls. Inmates fear both guards and prisoners, and some parolees charge that prison officials purposely use distrust, racial discord and prison power to maintain control within the prisons. A parolee describes an experience as follows:

> *One guy came up to my cell and said, "Hey, I hear there's some guys planning to fuck you. I can't tell you who they are, but I think I can stop them from doin' it, but they'll want some money. If you'll give me two bucks, I can stop 'em." And I knew what this guy is pullin'. . . . I just told him, "No," but I worried about it for a long time.*
>
> San Diego Parolee, 1970

One parolee says:

> *The events in California don't compare to the joints in
> Texas. I faced death so many times there . . . I was gagged,
> beat, drugged, stomped and everything.*
> *San Diego Parolee, 1970*

In recalling such experiences, the negative aspects may be exaggerated; nevertheless, these are the kinds of statements which were expressed when the parolees shared what stood out in their minds about the time they were in the joint.

Another 28% expressed ambivalent or neutral statements about their prison experience, e.g., "I settled down," "It woke me up," "I realized I had to make my own effort," and "I went to school." Many felt that the main thing one has to do is adjust to the way things are done in the prison.

In all, the parolees did not feel that there were adequate programs of rehabilitation within the prison. While the primary purpose of the prison is to keep a person in custody, most experts in the field of criminology agree that rehabilitation must be a part of the formal prison program if recidivism is to be reduced.

### Looking Ahead to Getting Out

Inmates look forward to the day when they will be released from prison. What they will experience upon release is secondary to their desire for freedom, although many of them know that it will not be easy. This attitude, general among the ex-offenders, is probably best expressed as follows:

> *Being in the penitentiary, you sit up there and you
> dream about what's going to happen when you get out.
> You expect everything to fall in place when you get out,
> but yet it don't fall in place like you want it to.*
> *San Diego Parolee, 1970*

Or, as another parolee describes it:

> *You know, when I first came out—I guess maybe every-
> body has this—they figure the whole world is gonna stop
> for them, and you think when you come back to your*

*hometown the brass bands are gonna play, and it's going*
*to be declared a national holiday, but it doesn't happen*
*that way.*

San Diego Parolee, 1970

While an inmate serves his sentence, he *may* be trained in a
trade, take credit courses, or receive guidance and counseling, but
none of these things are likely, for reasons ranging from reluctance on the part of the prisoner to insufficient opportunity for all.
Some believe—an idea inherited from the Puritan tradition—that
he will have served penance and have become penitent and re-
morseful while in prison, as the word "penitentiary" indicates. To
the contrary, he will probably have spent his time in prison
dreaming about what he will do when he gets out, dreams which
are often unrealistic.

*The first time a guy kind of sits back and goes on a fan-*
*tasy kick, like he's goin' to have money and broads and all*
*that sort of thing, but I knew what to expect this time. In*
*other words, you got to pick up the old lunch bucket and*
*go to work, and there's no moving mountains or glamour*
*or nothing like that.*

San Diego Parolee, 1970

Sometimes the prison experience makes an imprint upon the individual such that he will do everything in his power to avoid being
returned—his attitude will be changed.

*So I'm pretty sure I'll make it. What I want to do now is*
*completely different from what I wanted to do before I got*
*locked up. All I wanted to do was smoke dope then.*

San Diego Parolee, 1970

Another parolee, after spending 17 years off and on in prison, this
time says:

*No more hustlin'. Them days are over. The way I've*
*been livin' and the hard times that I've gone through. I*
*can't see turnin' back now . . . I can't see it no way!*

San Diego Parolee, 1970

For others there will be no change, and they intend to continue to commit crimes. In fact, "this belief in his own strong proclivity toward deviance is an important aspect in the thought processes of the criminal" (Irwin 1970:90), and probably an influence upon his behavior.

> *I expected a lot more temptation than I have had. I expected when I got out of here I would be thinking about burglarizing this place or knocking off that place, but I haven't had that. I was real surprised.*
> San Diego Parolee, 1970

**Getting Out**

Given the negative experience of prison, of being locked up for many years, it might be expected that the joy of being released would overshadow any initial difficulties and, at least for the first few days, parole would be a positive experience. But this is not usually so.

When the parolees were asked what it was like the first few days out, nearly half of them reported negative experiences. They described their experiences upon release as rough, a bummer, strenuous, a hassle, disappointing, same as before, confusing, and hard; they expressed feelings of seeming lost, lonesome, depressed, nervous, unsure, or paranoid. One parolee expressed it like this:

> *The best way to describe getting out is what it would be like for a cat that's been penned up all the time. Let it out and it sees a mouse, and it don't know whether to catch it or run from it. He's sort of lost.*
> San Diego Parolee, 1970

Thirty-four percent reported that the release experience was a generally positive one; it did feel good to be out, and being out is described as sweet, more beautiful than before, smooth, good, far out, etc.

Why isn't the release experience more positive and therefore a factor contributing to high morale and motivation that would help sustain the parolee through the transition from prison to after-prison life? The fact remains that upon release the parolee is immediately faced with the problems of providing the necessities of life—food, shelter, clothing, and work for himself. Most parolees spend a large proportion of their "walk-around" money for clothing of their own choosing and discard the clothes provided by the prison. Unless they have the help of others, they must obtain lodging, pay for their own meals, get to and from work, and make the $40 or $50 with which they typically leave the prison suffice until the first payday.

The majority of those released do not have the supportive interpersonal and material resources that most people would consider essential if they were to attempt a new life. And it is a new life. Consider the fact that many have been "out of touch" for years, isolated in prison from what has been going on in their home communities. Further, half of the parolees do not return to the communities from which they were sentenced. Only a quarter are married. Parole agents do not focus upon the first few days of release and the "emergency" funds available for parolees are very small. Prisoners look forward to getting out but they have little or no help and they have to "hit the streets running full tilt."

Chapter 4

# What Parolees Need

- *40% of the parolees report they are unemployed.*
- *30% of newly released parolees report unemployment.*
- *50% of parolees out two years report unemployment.*
- *70% of spontaneously expressed needs were physical/ material.*
- *Money, job, job training, and education were the highest ranked needs.*
- *Not using their ability, lack of money, and inadequate education were the three greatest concerns.*

## Hierarchy of Needs

The expressed needs of the parolees upon their release from prison match with Maslow's (1954) assertion that human beings can, under favorable conditions, experience and satisfy a hierarchy of needs. At the base of the hierarchy are the physiological needs, such as hunger, thirst, etc. Next in line are the safety needs, which include the opportunity to experience a sense of security, well-being, and the possibility of survival in one's environment. Belongingness and love needs are next highest in the hierarchy, and describe the yearning of the individual for affectionate relationships with people in general, for a place in a valued social group, and for the closeness of sharing with other human beings. Esteem needs are next, and include a broad set of desires for mastery, competence, confidence, independence, freedom, self-respect, self-esteem, respect and esteem from others, prestige, importance, appreciation, and so on. Finally, at the highest level of the hierarchy, is the need for self-actualization, which includes the desire and urge for maximizing one's creative, emotional, intellectual, interpersonal, unique, and experiential potentials. Few of the parolees expressed what could be considered higher level needs and probably because, according to Maslow, satisfaction of a lower need is seen as a prerequisite to the appearance and attempt to satisfy the next higher need.

## Pervasive Unemployment

One pervasive factor underlies the needs expressed. The reported rate of unemployment among the parolees is extremely high—40%. Unemployment has been and continues to be a serious national problem. The parolees talk about this and many of them say the stigma of being a con prevents them from obtaining employment. A steady job could probably have satisfied many of the other needs expressed.

It might be expected that the newly released parolees would be less likely to be employed than would those in the original sample who have been out an average of two years, but the reverse is true! Reported unemployment was 30% for *newly* released parolees and 50% for those who had been out for some time.

These figures indicate that the problem of unemployment is not a temporary condition that improves the longer the parolee is out. It may be that the lower unemployment rate for the newly released parolee reflects the fact that a common consideration for release from prison is having assured employment. However, many ex-cons and professionals believe that 90% of the jobs in release plans are "fictitious," i.e., promised by friends and relatives where in fact no "real" job exists.

The reason for unemployment does not appear to be because the parolees are looking for too highly skilled positions, because 50% said they would take anything. Most of the positions the parolees currently hold are skilled or unskilled labor. Unemployment not only means that the parolee is deprived of his physical and material needs but it also deprives him of an important source of primary group support, self-identity, and linkage to society. It is not possible from the existing data to determine why unemployment of parolees is so high, but the implications of high unemployment for return to crime are obvious. Glaser says that

"90% of reported felonies are property predations, so most of the recidivism of releasees may be regarded as a substitute for legitimate employment" (Glaser, 1972:104). A parolee sees the same problem:

> *When I first got out, I found it a little difficult to get a job, and as a matter of fact, I don't think I worked for the first six or eight months I was out. I was fortunate in that I had a little money. If I hadn't had this money it's just possible I would have gone back like some of these fellows that come out—no contacts, no connections— and they fall right back into crime.*
>
> San Diego Parolee, 1970

## Expressed Needs

When they were asked what kinds of things they had run up against when released, the parolees' statements were dominated by concern for their physical and material needs. In fact, over one-half of their comments centered around jobs, money, credit, debts, place to live, etc. Personal and social problems, such as meeting new people, being involved with drinking or drugs, and trouble in dealing with relatives, were the themes for about one-fourth of their responses. The remaining responses included "no problems" and general statements.

The parolees were asked to say, "I need," and complete the sentence as many times as they could. (The ex-offenders yielded an average of 5.6 responses each with a range of from 1-14.) As indicated in Table 1, the needs expressed by the ex-offenders were predominantly physical-material. Those needs were expressed both in absolute terms, e.g., "I need a job," and relative terms, e.g., "I need a better job." Employment, financial improvement, and transportation were the physical-material needs most frequently expressed, though "general assistance" accounted for several of the responses and included such expressed needs as: "counseling," "generally need help," "need a lot of things," etc. One parolee spelled out his reluctance to seek fulfillment of psychological needs:

> *If I openly admit that I need or want psychiatric help,*

*I'll have to go back in the joint to get it.*

*San Diego Parolee, 1970*

The "predominantly social needs" category and the "predominantly psychological needs" category were both powerfully expressed, however, by many of the ex-offenders.

Table 1

Need Response Categories for Ex-Offenders,
Percentage Responding
(N = 56)

| Needs | % | Total % |
|-------|---|---------|
| Predominantly physical/material needs | | 46 |
| Job | 12 | |
| Money | 12 | |
| General assistance | 8 | |
| Transportation | 6 | |
| Clothes | 4 | |
| Housing | 2 | |
| Medical/Dental | 2 | |
| Predominantly social needs | | 27 |
| General acceptance | 16 | |
| Friends | 5 | |
| Wife-Mate | 3 | |
| Family | 3 | |
| Predominantly psychological/personal needs | | 21 |
| Self-attribute needs | 16 | |
| Harm-avoidance needs | 3 | |
| Altruistic needs | 2 | |
| Other expressed needs | | 6 |
| Need nothing more | 3 | |
| Leisure | 2 | |
| Religion, parole modification and education | 1 | |

The parolees were also shown a list of 12 needs drawn in part from other studies of the offender, and were asked to place them in rank order with what they "do not have and need most" as Number 1. They were asked to rate each of the same needs in terms of how adequately they were being fulfilled, "below average, average and above average." The results of their responses are shown in Table 2.

Table 2

Rank Order of Needs and Adequacy of Need Fulfillment
as Indicated by the Parolees
(N=60)

| [a]Needs | Rank–Order | | | Adequacy | | |
|---|---|---|---|---|---|---|
| | Original Sample | New Parolees | Overall Total | Below Average | Average | Above Average |
| | | | | % | % | % |
| Education | 1 | 1 | 1 | 15 | 63 | 22 |
| Money | 2 | 2 | 2 | [b]53 | 37 | 10 |
| Job | 4 | 3 | 3 | 37 | 40 | 23 |
| Job Training | 3 | 4 | 4 | 33 | 35 | 32 |
| Circle of friends | 6 | 5 | 5 | 25 | 58 | 17 |
| Home/Shelter | 7 | 7 | 6 | 10 | 55 | 35 |
| Medical care | 10 | 8 | 7 | 23 | 50 | 27 |
| Recreational activities | 5 | 10 | 8 | 25 | 52 | 23 |
| Legal assistance | 9 | 11 | 9 | [b]50 | 42 | 8 |
| Sexual life | 12 | 6 | 10 | 20 | 53 | 27 |
| Dental care | 8 | 12 | 11 | 25 | 55 | 20 |
| Marriage/Home life | 11 | 9 | 12 | 13 | 60 | 27 |

[a]Not listed in order in which they appeared on interview schedule.
[b]Modal response is "Below Average" on these only. All other modal
responses are average.

Education, money and job were ranked first in order of priority,
according to Table 2. A rank-order correlation coefficient was
performed to measure the amount of agreement between the
needs of those just released (new parolees) and those who have
been out an average of two years (original sample).* The rank order of needs did not change over time and there was a high correlation (.71) between the needs of the minority and the white parolees. The high priority given education is accounted for by the
fact that education was ranked first by both blacks and browns,
and second by whites. The educational level of the blacks and
browns is only slightly higher (10.9 years) than the whites (10.6
years), but the minorities apparently experience the shortcomings
of a lower level of education to a greater extent than do the
whites.

_____

*A correlation of .64 was found between the 2 groups, when +1.00 is a perfect
positive correlation. With an N of 12 (ranks), if there is agreement in the rank
orders of a rho greater than .506, then the 2 rank orders are significantly corre-
lated (Guilford, 1956:549).

Correctional programs are not noted for stressing educational opportunities for ex-cons and the unanticipated emphasis that parolees gave to education requires further study. Education was not spontaneously mentioned in response to the unstructured questions but only when it appeared as a choice in the structured questions.

The parolees generally felt that their needs were filled in an average manner. On rating the adequacy of need fulfillment shown on Table 2, the modal response was "average" in all but two categories—money and legal assistance, in which they were "below average." The need for money has ranked among the first in all of the measures of needs, but the need for legal assistance has not occurred previously.

The needs of the parolees were approached in yet another manner, one that differed from the other questions and produced somewhat different results. This question focused on what the parolees were concerned with or worried about. The directions were as follows:

> *Below are listed 12 different things that people worry about or are concerned about from time to time. Please pick the 3 that you are most concerned about at the present time. Remember, look over the whole list of 12, and then pick the 3 that are of most concern to you right now.*

Their responses showed the concerns listed in Table 3, ordered by average response. The parolee's belief that he has a lot of ability that he is not using is expressed in other parts of the interviews and coincides with a desire for certain kinds of personal characteristics to help him to stay out of the joint, as discussed in the following section. Money and education rank high again, which is consistent with the findings in Table 2.

Table 3

Areas of Concern as Seen by the Parolees

| [a]Concerns | N | % |
|---|---|---|
| I have a lot of ability that I am not really using. | 36 | 20 |
| I don't have enough money. | 31 | 17 |
| My education isn't good enough. | 27 | 15 |
| I don't read enough. | 16 | 9 |
| I can't find steady work. | 16 | 9 |
| The people who make the decisions don't really care what my opinions are. | 12 | 7 |
| People in my family don't get along well. | 10 | 6 |
| I feel "cut off" from other people and things that are happening these days. | 9 | 5 |
| I don't have enough friends. | 7 | 4 |
| I think I could like myself more than I do. | 6 | 3 |
| I wish I had newer or better clothes. | 5 | 3 |
| The place I live in is bad news. | 3 | 2 |

[a]Not listed in order in which they appeared on interview schedule.
Each respondent chose three things about which he was most concerned.

The areas of concern can be grouped into physical/material, social relations, and personal characteristics. As indicated in Table 4, a different pattern emerges than for the results of questions that focused more directly on needs. The parolees' major areas of concern in this case were their personal characteristics followed by physical/material concerns and then social relations concerns. While the pattern differs, it is not inconsistent if the wording of the question shifted the parolees' thoughts to causal factors or longer range needs, as could be expected. To obtain better education and to use one's ability better are instrumental steps in solving physical/material problems.

In summary, the pattern of results indicates the saliency of physical/material needs, which would be expected by a group of men 40% of whom are unemployed. Both conventional wisdom and motivation theory argue that the difficult process of social and personal adjustment is handicapped if not completely blocked for many parolees if they must scramble to meet their basic physical needs.

In line with Maslow's reasoning and the results of this chapter, programs for rehabilitating the ex-offender must give satisfaction of physical needs top priority. However, it should not be overlooked that the results indicate that a wide variety of needs are experienced by the parolees.

Table 4

Areas of Concern as Seen by the Parolees

| Concerns | Responses | Total |
|---|---|---|
| Personal characteristics | | 85 |
| Not using ability | 36 | |
| Education not good enough | 27 | |
| Don't read enough | 16 | |
| Could like myself more | 6 | |
| Physical/material needs | | 55 |
| Not enough money | 31 | |
| Out of work | 16 | |
| Need better clothes | 5 | |
| Place I live is bad | 3 | |
| Social relations | | 38 |
| Decision-makers unconcerned about me | 12 | |
| Family doesn't get along well | 10 | |
| Feel cut off | 9 | |
| Don't have enough friends | 7 | |

## Summary

Many of the respondents virtually pleaded for primary group support and for social "understanding" of their perplexity and their difficulties. This was especially apparent in the relatively large percentage of "general acceptance" responses. "General acceptance" reflected such expressed needs as understanding, love, respect, etc. They are also looking for a social anchoring. Those ex-offenders who expressed psychological needs such as self-attribute needs, called, in particular, for help which would provide them with the kinds of psychological characteristics allowing them to "make it" in the "straight" world. They wanted to be shown ways to understand themselves, to experience pride in self, to "get their heads straight," and to "hang in there when the going got rough," etc. In short, they wanted to acquire those psychological characteristics, whatever they were, that would keep them out of the "joint." They were also looking for a rewarding sense of identity.

Although satisfaction of physical/material needs deserves first priority, it would be shortsighted to overlook the wide variety of needs and fail to design rehabilitation programs that can assist the ex-offender to move progressively up the hierarchy of needs. The parolees are clearly saying they need help, as in the following quote:

> *I was 39 years old before I went to prison. Before that, I was a "lock 'em up and throw the key away" guy. Now that I've come out, I have a lot more compassion and feeling for people that are in. I believe the only way that we're ever going to break this cycle of "out the door and back in again" is to help these people when they get out.*
>
> San Diego Parolee, 1970

Another parolee says: "I'm hungry for human help, that's what I'm hungry for. And I'm gettin' it just little by little, inch by inch, but I'm gettin' it."

It should be underscored that the needs expressed in the interviews of the parolees who had been out two years did not differ in significant ways from those just released. Apparently nothing significant happens during two years of parole to change parolees' needs. The physical needs most often expressed are money, job, and education, all of which are interrelated. One does not get the impression in the analysis that the money they desire is "easy money" but rather that most of them are willing to work for it. Nearly all of them expect that a job will be difficult to find, and that being an ex-con can deter one from obtaining a job.

> *I knew more or less that it would be difficult because I'd always read that men with a criminal past would find it difficult to fit back into society, because it seems everybody wants to give you a blast on the chin rather than give you a helping hand.*
>
> San Diego Parolee, 1970

In all, the parolees' needs did not seem unreasonable, but many cannot find ways by which to meet them. One parolee says, simply, "I find that my wants exceed my means of getting them." For others, past experience has allowed them to be realistic:

> *Like I said, I don't really have those wild ideas of needing a great wad of loot or anything, and I'm not serenading a bunch of broads or anything of that nature, so I'm*

*not really pushed out of shape about anything.*
                              *San Diego Parolee, 1970*

The parolee above has a realistic view, but it can readily be understood that most of them would be "pushed out of shape" when 40% are unemployed, almost all are low on money, several have a feeling of being under-educated, and many feel unaccepted by society.

# Chapter 5

# High Hopes

The parolees in this study seem to share middle-class attitudes and ambitions but lack resources—money, job, education and interpersonal and social support—to obtain them, as this chapter will point out. In this sense, at least some of the parolees can be understood in light of Merton's theory of anomie. Merton concentrated on the social order, stressing that ambition to achieve unattainable objectives is induced by the social structure (Clinard, 1964:11). He said that two elements of American social structure, namely, means and goals, are often dichotomized, and an individual usually adjusts to this dichotomy in one of five ways. *Conformity,* the first, is the acceptance of both the cultural goals and the institutionalized means for achieving them; *innovation* is the acceptance of goals, but rejection of the means for achieving them; *ritualism* is the rejection of the cultural goals but the acceptance of the means; *retreatism* is the rejection of both the goals and the means; *rebellion,* finally, is the rejection of both means and goals, substituting new goals and new means for achieving them. In other words, these five varieties of adjustment involve acceptance or rejection, alternately, of goals or means. An example of innovation (usually criminal behavior) would be an upstanding businessman and civic leader (accepted American goal), supplementing his regular business income with resources from drug traffic (unacceptable means).

Cloward and Ohlin (Bordua, 1962:298) say that American culture actually makes it morally mandatory that everyone seek success but the socially acceptable means of reaching the goals (the legitimate opportunities) are differentially distributed—thus their "differential opportunity" model of delinquency, i.e., a lower-class teenager steals a car. Gibbons (1965:47) says, in fact, that much of American criminality is carried on by "normal" persons who are pursuing conventional goals by illicit means, and the causes of the deviation are located in social class relationships, family and peer interactions, and contacts with agencies of social control.

For the parolee recently released from prison, there are the "combined effects of social rejection by being labeled a criminal, incarceration with its attendant experience of degradation, and difficulty in adjusting to lawful community life in the absence of attractive enough conventional goals . . . ." (Dembo, 1971:354). The concept of differential opportunity and the incongruity between means available to the parolee and the goals he desires may have contributed to his crimes preceding incarceration. These same factors usually continue to exist upon his release. His behavior patterns upon release may or may not include committing further crimes, but clearly a future determinant of his behavior is how he sees his present situation in relation to his conception of an ideal life or what he expects of himself.

Cantril (1965:22) devised a scale to measure level of aspiration and expectations which he calls the Self-Anchoring Striving Scale. This scale was used with the parolees. A respondent is shown a picture of a ladder with steps from 0 to 10, with 0 being the worst possible life and 10 being the best possible life. It is a self-defined continuum, which is based on the individual's own assumptions, goals, values, and perceptions. He is asked where he sees himself now, where he saw himself five years ago and where he sees himself five years from now. For the parolees, an additional question was asked: "Where do you see most other ex-cons on this ladder now?"

The average ratings on the ladder could range from 0 to 10. The mean ratings of the American people surveyed by Cantril (N=2696) and the parolees surveyed in this study (N=60) are shown in Table 5. The American Public sample and the parolees differ significantly on all ladder ratings at the level of .01. (Any differences between means above 1.01 are significant at the level of .01.)*

## Table 5
### Self-Anchoring Ladder
### Level of Aspiration

| Average Step on Ladder | Parolees | American Public |
|---|---|---|
| Five years ago | 3.1 | 5.9 |
| Present | 5.5 | 6.6 |
| Five years ahead | 8.8 | 7.8 |
| Other cons at present | 4.0 | |

Most of the parolees were in prison five years ago, so it is to be expected that the mean rating on the ladder would be lower than that of the American Public. At present, the average step for the parolees is lower than for the general public, probably because one-half of the parolees had been out of prison for less than two months. The parolees' levels of aspiration for five years from now are higher, however, than for the general public.

For further analysis, Cantril (1965:375) classified the mean ladder ratings of the American public for the past, present and future on the major variables of sex, age, education, economic level, class, race, religion and occupation, with subcategories within each. The disparity between the parolees' present and past levels on the ladder, as compared to their future aspirations, can best be exemplified through a comparison with each of these subgroups. In looking at the past, the parolees place themselves at 3.1 (lower than any other subsegment). The lowest mean ladder ranking for any category of the American public is 5.2 (rated by those 21 to 29 years of age). The lower-middle class is the next lowest group for

---

*For the American Public sample, differences between average ladder ratings of .2 are significant at the .05 level. For the parolees, differences between ladder ratings of 1.41 are significant at .01. Therefore, the means indicated in the tables above are found to be significant for the American Public sample at the .05 level and for the parolees at the .01 level. According to Cantril (1965:362), standard deviations were calculated for a sample of 444 separate ladder ratings in the American study. A plot of the number of respondents per rating (N) against $SD^2/N$ indicated the limits within which 95% of all values lay for a selected range of Ns. Using these lower and upper values, differences between means required at three levels of significance ($p < .1$, $p < .05$, and $p < .01$) were calculated.

five years ago (5.3), still nowhere near as low as the parolees saw themselves. Again, this is an expected finding because most of them were in prison.

Looking at the present rankings, the parolees see themselves at a mean step of 5.5. Only two of Cantril's subsegments place themselves lower than this: non-white (5.3) and the lower class (4.6). All of the educational subsegments are at a higher level: college graduates (6.9), high school graduates (6.7), and grammar school (6.2). So the parolees, with two exceptions, see themselves significantly lower at present than all other subsegments of American society.

When rating themselves for the future, however, the picture drastically changes, as the parolees see themselves *higher* than any other subsegment listed. The parolees place themselves on step 8.8. The group within Cantril's sample which comes closest to that level is the Jewish group (8.6), followed by the college-educated (8.5), the upper class (8.3), the middle economic group (8.2), and professional and white-collar workers (8.2). So the parolees move from aspirations similar to those of the young, lower-class and non-white to those of the highest echelon within a very few years. This high level of aspiration suggests unrealistic expectations, since the parolees' median education is less than high school completion and 40% are presently unemployed.

**Feelings Of Effectiveness**

How effective or powerful a person feels also contributes to that individual's relation to society and what he believes he can achieve. The Personal Efficacy Scale was administered to the parolees in order to assess this characteristic. It is a series of five items, in a forced choice situation, consisting of two statements each. The respondent is asked to choose which of the two statements best reflects how he feels. One of the statements indicates a feeling of effectiveness, the other does not. For each set of statements, a score of 1 was received if a positive statement was selected, and a score of 0 was received if a negative statement was chosen. The highest possible score is 5 (feels most effective) and the lowest possible is 0 (feels least effective). The mean score on the Personal Efficacy Scale obtained by the parolees was 2.65. Two samples of Berkeley students, male and female (N = 47 and

N = 19), were administered the same test and achieved mean scores of 2.08 and 1.95, respectively. For the same study (Berzon, 1968) two groups of male inmates at the Barrett Honor Camp, each with 21 subjects, were administered this test and obtained mean scores of 2.14 and 2.57. While much more adequate comparative information would be needed to substantiate any definite conclusion, it would appear that parolees do not suffer from strong feelings of ineffectiveness.

### A Middle-Class Orientation

A feeling of effectiveness is found in the parolees' expectations of success on parole. The parolees were asked: "Do you think you're going to make it?" (on parole), and only one parolee said, "No," that he would not make it. The interviewer believed that this person was already "on the run" at the time of the interview. In short, the parolees feel effective and expect to make it despite their difficulties.

The parolees' ideas and plans for success on parole stress struggle, hard work and self-restraint as shown on Table 6. Being successful was most often viewed as difficult—a struggle. The parolees frequently saw "not doing certain things" as a means of succeeding, and also practicing self-control. Several parolees said that if they lowered their aspirations they would probably not get into trouble again. This orientation towards life is consistent with

Table 6
Ideas for "Making It"
As Seen by the Parolees
*(N = 63)

| Ideas | N | % |
|---|---|---|
| I will struggle and work hard. | 17 | 27 |
| I will not do those things which eventually led to my going to prison. | 14 | 22 |
| I will practice self-control. | 10 | 16 |
| I will get along on what I have, lower my aspirations. | 8 | 13 |
| I will stay close to the parole plan. | 5 | 8 |
| I will accept help. | 4 | 6 |
| I will wait to see what happens. | 3 | 5 |
| I will hide and defend myself from others. | 2 | 3 |

*Multiple responses.

American middle-class values and it is indeed this group with which the parolees compare themselves.

In fact, the parolees were asked: "With what group of people did you compare yourself when talking about whether or not your needs were being fulfilled?" The answer most frequently given was the "average" or "middle-class" person. This supports the belief, expressed in other portions of this chapter, that the needs and values of the ex-cons are possibly no different from those of the average law-abiding person. The popular myth that the criminal has rejected society's values, that he is a "public enemy" in the sense of not sharing the orientation towards the world of the law-abiding general public is contradicted by these results. As one con who has been out two and a half years and has not been able to find steady work expressed it:

> *It's always been astonishing to me to see the cars going down the freeway to work in the morning and then at 4:30 in the afternoon. If a man's never experienced a steady job like this, it makes him want to get into the scene and join the crowd. I've looked at this and I've sort of wanted to become a part of the community.*
>
> San Diego Parolee, 1970

Although further study would be necessary before a definite assertion could be made, it would seem very probable that a high but unrealistic level of aspiration can encourage people to act outside of the law in order to achieve their goals. A rehabilitation model to "resocialize" inmates or parolees should consider, as indicated by this study, that the parolees tend already to accept the values of the larger society, and they aspire toward acceptable societal goals. The problem seems to be that the parolees do not have the necessary resources to reach their goals by legitimate means, and the alternatives which they select to reach them are often different from those of the "law-abiding" citizen.

The parolees in this study have a considerable number of needs—physical and social—yet they have high hopes for their futures. The question remains: How will they obtain such resources as jobs, money, education, and social support, which will allow them to legitimately attain their goals? As long as an employer refuses to hire an ex-convict, or the general public says, "I don't want to live next to one," it is not likely that the parolee can attain his goals in an acceptable manner. A parolee, recently released, summarizes this dilemma:

> *Okay, so if I'm no longer a criminal, why do I have to be an ex-convict? Why can't I go back to society in the same capacity as I came out of society? Why do they have to say, "Now we're tattooing you with this label. You're an ex-convict for two and a half years." He is paroled, but not free of the label.*

Chapter 6

# Relation To Others

Results from the previous chapters have indicated the scarcity of interpersonal and social support for the parolees: 72% do not have the support of a marital arrangement; 73% have been away from the community three or more years; 50% return to a community other than the one they were sentenced from; 40% are unemployed and do not have the support of a work group.

Because an individual's associations are an important factor in his orientation toward the world, we asked the parolees about their informal associations with friends, relatives, and neighbors. The results are presented in Table 7, where parolee responses are compared with those of the general population. Even though some parolees commented on the importance of the family, it did not rank as high in frequency of contact as might be expected. The comparison with the sample of the general population in a Detroit study conducted by Axelrod (1964: 722-729) yields results with implications for rehabilitation programs. The general population rank-ordered frequencies of contact with others as follows: 1) relatives, 2) friends, and 3) neighbors. For the parolees, the rank order frequency of contact is quite different: 1) friends, 2) neighbors, and 3) relatives. Axelrod says that relatives are an important source of companionship and mutual support, judging from the frequency of contact. He says further that the rank order has held true for almost every important segment of population that he has studied. The only exception Axelrod found were groups with high status, high income or college education. He suggests that education and sophistication may give these individuals their own resources for integration, which the general population receive from their families.

### Table 7
Frequency of Association with Informal Groups
A Comparison of Detroit Area Sample of General Population
and San Diego Parolee Population
Percentage Responding

| Frequency of Association | Relatives | | Friends | | Neighbors | |
|---|---|---|---|---|---|---|
| | Parolees | General Pop. | Parolees | General Pop. | Parolees | General Pop. |
| At least once a week | 37 | 49 | 67 | 28 | 42 | 29 |
| At least once a month | 18 | 25 | 18 | 18 | 13 | 18 |
| Less often, Never | 45 | 22 | 13 | 31 | 53 | 50 |
| Other, Not ascertained | 0 | 4 | 2 | 4 | 2 | 3 |

In that case, the markedly different results obtained for the parolees in this study merit consideration. The possibility exists that the parolees are not, in fact, receiving as much support and companionship as may be necessary for them to maintain feelings of integration with society, and other portions of the study have indicated that they do not have other resources, i.e., money, status and education, to replace familial support. At the same time, it is possible, though not likely, that friends and neighbors may replace the warmth usually received from the family within the general population. It is more likely that the parolees simply do not have, either upon release or later, the essential ties, connections, and support necessary for successful integration and reentry into society.

The greater frequency of contact with friends and neighbors reported by the parolees as compared to the general population can be seen as a reaching out for primary support to overcome their relative lack of internal or familial resources. If the friends and neighbors are oriented to the criminal subculture, then the result of deficient primary support from relatives can lead to increased probability of recidivism, as indicated by the theory of differential association. The theory says that "a person becomes delinquent because of an excess of definitions favorable to violation of law over definitions unfavorable to violation of law" (Sutherland & Cressey 1960: 430). These definitions are most commonly obtained through association and interaction with significant others. Becker (1963: 31) similarly says, "The individual learns, in short, to participate in a subculture organized around the particular deviant activity." We do not have data on the background of the friends and neighbors to whom the parolees refer in their response to the informal association question. However, their association with criminals was explored in a series of questions. The questions and results appear in Table 8, a modification of Short's scale (1966).

Sixty-five percent of the parolees said that there was crime and delinquency committed in the community in which the parolees grew up, with all of the browns indicating that there was. Nearly half of the parolees said that they had friends who were juvenile delinquents; again, the browns had the greatest percentage indicating this. Over half of the parolees also indicate that they knew cons before going into the joint. The amount of association indicated by the parolees drops when they are asked about long-time friends (30%) and is considerably less since their release.

Even though there are no comparative data available, the theory of differential association receives support by the data presented above. Obviously the data are not conclusive; a sample of the general population would be necessary to determine the average degree of association with which this group could be com-

Table 8

Positive (Yes) Responses Regarding Differential Association
Percentage Responding, by Ethnicity

| Component of Differential Association | Whites (N = 37) | Blacks (N = 11) | Browns (N = 12) | Total (N = 60) |
|---|---|---|---|---|
| Delinquency committed by young people in the community in which you grew up | 57 | 55 | 100 | 65 |
| Most or several first best friends were juvenile delinquents | 32 | 36 | 83 | 43 |
| Knew cons before going into the joint | 54 | 64 | 50 | 55 |
| Most or several friends known for the longest time are cons | 16 | 45 | 58 | 30 |
| Most or several friends you've been associated with since release are cons | 22 | 27 | 50 | 28 |

pared, and the causative influence of the association cannot be confirmed unless other influencing factors are isolated.

Indications of differential association were found throughout the 1200 pages of interviews. Eight of the 60 respondents specifically attributed "going to prison" to the exterior environment and associations, saying "environment," "the street scene," or "the crowd I hung around with." Two of the parolees said that the way they will "make it" on parole is to stay away from old associates; so for some, the problem, in their view, was indeed their associates and their environment. The vignettes presented in Chapter 1 alluded to criminal associates' influences both before and after prison.

The ex-offenders are sometimes keenly aware of the influence, as found when a parolee was asked what led him to going to the prison:

> *Wrong association with the wrong people led me to the joint. I was thrown out of home when I was 17. I've been in and out of jail, juvenile hall, juvenile camp, had a broken family and things like that.*
>
> San Diego Parolee, 1970

One obvious problem in measuring differential association after release from prison is that a condition of parole is as follows: "You must avoid association with former inmates of penal institutions unless specifically approved by your Parole Agent and you must avoid association with individuals of bad reputation."* Since this is a parole condition and a violation could mean being returned to prison, it is likely that there is a consistent underestimation of *current* association with cons. There is no reason to believe the *past* association would be underestimated, however.

Cressey (1966: 469) has based a recommendation upon the principle that people become criminals principally because of association with other criminals or those with criminal beliefs, and that they have isolated themselves from groups whose behaviors and attitudes are primarily anti-criminal. "If criminals

---

*Taken from "Conditions of Parole," State of California, Adult Authority, Parole and Community Services Division, Sacramento, California, CDC-1515.

are to be changed, either they must become members of anti-criminal groups, or their present pro-criminal group relations must be changed."

Cressey (1966: 471) suggests the practice of "retroflexive reformation"; a criminal is changed by working with non-criminals to help other criminals. We found that nine ex-cons in this study were working with "squares" to help other ex-cons, which is an example of retroflexive reformation. Eleven parolees were helping ex-cons, but not working with squares to do it, i.e., helping them find jobs on their own; and 33 were not helping other ex-cons in any way. These responses included both formal and informal "working with" ex-cons. The parolees were asked if they were involved in any rehabilitation groups, and only 15% said that they were. While this is a small percentage it is likely that it will increase over the next few years with the introduction of the "self-help" concept, in which ex-cons join together to help other ex-cons. The rehabilitation group most frequently mentioned by the parolees was Community Achievement Improvement Group (CAIG), a group of volunteers, often ex-cons, who go into the prison and work with the inmate before he is released on parole to help smooth the transition to the community. Referring to this experience, one individual said:

> *If somebody comes in who's been in the joint—spent a good amount of time in there—knows what's happening and got out and made it, then I look up to him more, relate to him better.*
>
> *San Diego Parolee, 1970*

Other parolees expressed a desire to relate to other ex-cons who are "making it."

> *I imagine everyone coming out wants to make it, and so you look towards the people who have been in that are making it now, and these people are what helped me the most.*
>
> *San Diego Parolee, 1970*

It is likely that the social trend of people with similar problems, stigmas, or goals banding together will continue and the ex-cons will no doubt be a part of this movement. Such a movement will necessitate a formal recognition by authorities and perhaps a subsequent change in "Conditions of Parole" which currently prohibit association with other offenders. Irwin (1970: 130) says that parole agents express concern over the fact that ex-convicts are congregating and associating in unsupervised settings. In some places, it is encouraged though, and in future years we are likely to see more of the ex-offender groups involved in helping other offenders.

Chapter 7

# The Parolee's Self-Concept

The felon has a high probability of rarely having experienced a sense of belongingness in an acceptable social world. If he experienced any sense of social solidarity with others in criminal acts, that solidarity probably was disrupted by arrest, conviction and imprisonment. Even if he did experience a sense of belongingness during incarceration, release on parole into society at large probably again dislocated him (Glaser, 1964). Addressing himself to the felon's problem of reentry into the "straight" world, Irwin (1970: 117) writes:

> Not only does the world seem strange; the self loses its distinctiveness. Not only does the person find the new setting strange and unpredictable, and not only does he experience anxiety and disappointment from his inability to function normally in this strange setting, but he loses a grip on his profounder meanings, his values, goals, conceptions of himself.
>
> In this situation, planned, purposeful action becomes extremely difficult. Such action requires a definite sense of self, a relatively clear idea of one's relation to other things, and some sense of one's direction or goal. All of these tend to become unravelled in a radical shift of settings.

Mead (in Strauss, 1964) has written that individuals who are experiencing social and interpersonal instability tend, as an adjustment mechanism, to make themselves objects—to become self-evaluative, reflective, introspective. Since the social world the parolee perceives lacks stability, he essentially declares a degree of independence from it, and in a sense makes himself more of an island. He will continue to do this as long as it is functional, until he finds a satisfactory niche in a relatively predictable, welcoming, and rewarding social situation.

Stability of self-concept and the degree to which perception of self fits with the perceptions of significant others contributes to the well-being of the individual. If he manifests a relatively stable self-concept, the assumption generally is that he sees himself as comfortably belonging in an acceptable social world. Furthermore, that social world, as the individual perceives it, is itself stable, dependable, and valued by significant others.

The individual's self-concept can be shaken if those interpersonal and structural networks upon which he depends for definition of self are destroyed, disrupted, or made unacceptable. Under such conditions, his social and psychological anchorings become loosened, his accustomed self-concept no longer is lodged in his social world, and he may experience confusion, conflict, anxiety, frustration, and rigidity in adaptive modes. Examples of the kind of cataclysmic conditions which could produce such disruption of self-concept are: community physical disaster (Taylor, Zurcher & Key, 1970); family disruption by death or separation (Davis, 1963); sudden cultural relocation (Handlin, 1951); and socialization into the military (Zurcher, 1967) and into other total institutions such as prisons and asylums (Goffman, 1961).

It is also possible that self-concept, at least a self-concept which functions well in the "dominant" and "majority" social world, has never developed in a given individual. That is, the kinds of socialization processes he has experienced have developed in him a perception of self which includes the label "deviant," "minority," or some other alienative term. Other instabilities of self-concept might have developed by the individual's rejection of unacceptable socializing agents, or the general rejection of, or rejection by, the social system which supports socialization.*

Self-concept has been measured by social scientists in several

---

*For a general review of socialization as a process, including socialization in prisons, see Goslin (1969).

different ways (Wylie, 1961). One of the more popular measures, at least for research purposes, has been the Twenty Statements Test (TST) developed by Kuhn and McPartland (1954). The TST is an open-ended, relatively unstructured, paper and pencil instrument which elicits indices of self-concept from the respondent by asking him to answer, twenty times, the question, "Who am I?" Typically, the respondent is given a blank sheet of paper, asked to write the numbers one to twenty down the page, and then asked:

> Please write twenty answers to the simple question, "Who am I?" Just give twenty different answers to this question. Answer as if you were giving the answers to yourself, not to somebody else. Write the answers in the order that they occur to you. Don't worry about logic or "importance." Go along fairly fast, for time is limited. (Kuhn & McPartland, 1954:69)

Because the TST was administered in the present study as part of an extensive and structured interview procedure, the respondents were asked to answer the "Who am I?" question verbally, and to give as many responses as they wished. The TST responses, along with the rest of the structured interview, were tape-recorded.

There are several protocols for scoring the TST.* The protocol used in the present study was developed by McPartland, Cumming, and Garretson (1961) and establishes four categories for TST responses. Each of the categories represents a discrete grouping along a spectrum of self-identifying references, at a different level of abstraction from social experience. The categories and their analytical contents were:

> *"A" statements:* The most concrete level of reference which we distinguish presents the self as a physical entity (I am six feet tall, I weigh 170 pounds) or as an identity card does (age, sex, home address, eye color, hair color, and the like). We designate this class of self-identi-

---

*See, for example: Kuhn, 1960; Kuhn & McPartland, 1954; McPartland, Cumming & Garretson, 1961; McPartland & Cumming, 1958; Schmitt, 1966; Schwirian, 1964; and Spitzer, 1969. Other scoring variations are presented in "Manual for the Twenty Statements Problem," by S. Spitzer, 1965.

fications "A" and relate it theoretically to experiences of
self as a concrete organism with, at best, indirect reference to interpersonal transactions . . . the notion of self
reported in the concrete class of "A" statements is a
physical organism moving in space and time without
reference to, or involvement in, social relations or socially consequential action . . . "A" self-identifications
imply no others although they certainly present the self
as a social object. (These will be referred to as self-iden-
tification statements.)

*"B" statements:* The letter "B" designates statements
which abstract institutionalized statuses or roles as self-
identifying references and, therefore, imply "generalized other" or institutional patterns. Examples are: "I
am a student" (related to some educational organization
and through it to others in their various statuses in that
organization) . . . . We also use this category to include
statements which give status-like form to less clearly institutionalized self-references, e.g., "I am a lover" . . . .
"B" statements generally support inferences to experience of the self as involved in structured interpersonal
relations, as governed by a web of rights and duties, as
related to others through the mediation of internalized
norms. (These will be referred to as role-identity statements.)

*"C" statements:* The "C" category includes statements
which abstract characteristic ways of acting, feeling, or
responding in social interaction. "I am moody sometimes," "I like to be with people" . . . . The *others* implicit
in this kind of statement are not generalized into institutionalized patterns or abstract rules of conduct;
rather, other people and other objects appear as individual preferences or dislikes, or as sources of particula-
rized approval, support, agreement, enjoyment, or an-
tagonism. The identities presented in "C" statements
are not found by institutional context but rather are "sit-
uation-free" personal characteristics which are, nevertheless, normatively governed, and communicable in
the terms of ordinary discourse. "C" statements have

the common characteristic that they support inference to an experience of self as a person interacting more or less directly with other persons with a minimum of institutional mediation, but within normative limits and generally toward consensually supported goals. (These will be referred to as socially-unconnected statements.)

*"D" statements:* The letter "D" designates the fourth category of self-identifying statements. That category subsumes statements which abstract social experience in terms which imply no particular context, act or attitude of interactive consequence, or which so remove the self from interactive commitment as to be ambiguous or nondifferentiating, e.g., "I hope for the best for all," "I would like to try to be better." "D" statements support inference to experience which transcends human social action or interaction, e.g., "I am one with God" . . . or which negate personal commitment, e.g., "I am just one among billions." The *internalized others* implicit in "D" statements about the self are transcendental ("the cosmos" or "mankind") rather than "generalized" in the Meadian sense, and float beyond the possibility of consensual validation or even verifiable communication . . . . (These will be referred to as abstract statements.)

Viewed together, the A, B, C, D categories of self-identifying statements represent a spectrum which runs from conceptions of the self as a physical structure in time and space (category A), through conceptions of the self as existing in social structures (category B), and as a social interactor abstracted from social structures (category C), to conceptions of the self abstracted from physical being, from social structure, and from social interaction (category D). (McPartland, Cumming, & Garretson, 1961: 114-116)

We expected that ex-offenders, compared with other groups, would report more socially-unconnected responses. That is, they would be more self-evaluative, and in general would manifest a relative absence of stability of social anchoring and identification with social institutions. To get a broader picture of the components of ex-offender self-concept, for analytical exploration, the following additional response categories were added to the socially unconnected statements: self-derogation (Salisbury, 1963); ambition (Kuhn, 1960); anxiety about the future; criticism of the "system"; pessimism; and optimism.

The ex-offenders yielded an average of 8.6 TST responses, with a range of from 2 to 33. Table 9 reveals that the ex-offenders were predominantly socially unconnected in their TST responses. That is, the majority of their TST responses fell into the C category. Indeed, there were strikingly more socially unconnected responses among the parolees than in any other groups available for comparison, with the exception of the dissident priests.* According to the theory upon which the TST is based, the ex-offenders, when contrasted illustratively with the other respondent groups, manifested a relative lack of social anchoring, and a relative self-evaluative and searching "turning inward." Individuals who give predominantly socially unconnected responses may be governed by normative limits and act generally in accordance with consensually supported goals, but experience themselves as interacting with others under minimal institutional mediation. Such individuals are relatively situation free—rather loosely involved in social structure. They seem to be looking, within themselves and about their social world, for anchoring in an acceptable group, but are not quite certain what that group might be or if they will be accepted by such a group.

The ex-offender TST responses most resembled those of the dissident priests (Schneider & Zurcher, 1970). In some ways the social situation of the dissident priests and the ex-offenders were similar. The priests had lost, at least temporarily, their sense of social anchoring. They had perceived the church, that social system to which they had previously committed themselves and with

---

*These comparisons are, at best, illustrative only. The TSTs in those studies where the respondents were dissident priests (Schneider & Zurcher, 1970), former mental patients (Hartley, 1968a), mental patients (McPartland, Cumming, & Garretson, 1961), random college sample (Hartley, 1968b), middle-class adults and lower-class adults (McPartland & Cumming, 1958) were administered according to the traditional paper and pencil, twenty response procedure. Our TST data, as described above, were gathered verbally and with no specific number of responses being requested.

which they previously had been identified, to be now unacceptable. A disparity had grown up between their self-concept and their perception of the social institution upon which that self-concept had in good part been based previously. By choice, then, they rejected their social anchoring in the church social system and were acutely experiencing the psychological impact of having cast themselves adrift from previously supportive social moorings.

Table 9
Modal TST Categories ( % ) for Ex-Offenders
and Other Sample Groups

| Sample Groups | % (A-Mode) Self-Identity | % (B-Mode) Role-Identity | % (C-Mode) Socially Un-connected | % (D-Mode) Abstract |
|---|---|---|---|---|
| Ex-Offenders (N = 58) | 0 | 3 | 77 | 20 |
| Dissident Priests (N = 24) | 0 | 4 | 83 | 13 |
| Former Mental Patients (N = 146) | 8 | 18 | 31 | 42 |
| Mental Patients (N = 100) | 21 | 15 | 31 | 33 |
| Random College Sample (N = 165) | 2 | 51 | 31 | 16 |
| "Middle-Class" Adults (N = 137) | 3 | 65 | 27 | 5 |
| "Lower-Class" Adults (N = 36) | 0 | 33 | 53 | 14 |

It is not so clear, as it was with the dissident priests, that the reason the ex-offenders were predominantly unconnected was that they had rejected a previously acceptable social anchoring. It may well be that the ex-offenders have never in their lives experienced that social anchoring.

Another interpretation might be that the ex-offenders at one time did have a keen sense of social anchoring (and might have responded by identifying with the social structure), but this identification changed during imprisonment. A third view might suggest that their release from prison cast them into a confusing social world which itself made them feel unconnected. A further interpretation, fitting in part with those just mentioned, would suggest that most of the ex-offenders came from "lower-class" origins, and thus to some extent were influenced by these kinds of social factors. Table 9 shows that "lower-class" adults recorded a large percentage of socially unconnected responses, a finding which McPartland and Cumming (1958) suggest was generated by a tendency of "lower-class" respondents to have looser involvement in institutionalized social relations, less activity in voluntary associations, and disadvantages in competition for power and prestige in such arenas as school and work. Whatever the reason, it is dramatically apparent that most of the ex-offenders responded to the TST with statements that indicated they were not anchored to society's institutions.

Hartley (1968b) has indicated that such an individual has difficulty in adjusting to the social institutions of society at large. He has difficulty taking his place in complex organizations, in schools, and in interacting with typical middle-class America, in contrast to someone who has a self-concept that clearly is located in and identified with the dominant set of societal social roles and social institutions. The individual who responds with role-identity statements is described as behaving in socially effective ways and as being responsive to the role requirements of the social structure in which he comfortably operates. The self is conceived as existing in the social structure, and implies a "generalized other," which most nearly coincides with the demands of the organizational situation (Hartley 1968b). Yet the ex-offender, clearly and for whatever reason, is a more socially unconnected individual, who is cast out into a world where he is expected to identify himself and his role in relation to the larger social structure. Apparently prison, no matter what its socialization goals, does not produce individuals who can readily adapt to society. At least, their responses imply they are not anchored in society. The post-release procedures do not appear to provide the individual with acceptable or accepting social anchoring either. Consequently, he is cast adrift in what must appear to him to be a confusing, rejecting, and hostile social environment.

The response tendencies indicated by essentially socially unconnected statements are not necessarily unhealthy. To the contrary, there are times when it is extremely adaptive to turn within one's self, to remove one's self from an unacceptable social anchoring, and to begin searching for new social "turf." There are times when this kind of profile reflects the best possible adaptation to the current social situation. However, it seems that the ex-offenders would actually *prefer* to be able to evolve the kind of self-concept that others have, which would allow them to take their place in the dominant social world where the individual relates to organizations and social institutions. If prison and the traditional post-release procedures do not prepare them for such a world, then what can help them develop a self-concept which articulates more completely and fully with the "straight" world?

Many of the ex-offenders gave strong indications of intention to "make it in the straight world," to find some way to "get themselves straight," and to learn how to "fit in" with society at large. Very few of them were self-derogatory, anxious about the future, or critical of the establishment. They seemed to be searching for some place to take a social stand, where they would be accepted and understood, and where they could "make out" like other human beings who did not happen to be ex-offenders. But they didn't know where to take that stand, nor how to take it. Most of their frustration and bitterness seemed to be directed at the confusion of their own perception of self and their inability to find a relatively clear and rewarding path in society. Some of them were anxious that if such a path did not soon appear, they would find themselves back in "the joint."

Chapter 8

# Summary And Conclusions

Certain overall characteristics of the 60 parolees show that they are different from the general population: 37% are black or brown; 50% have not finished high school; 72% are not married; 40% are unemployed. Their prison experiences are lengthy: 73% have served more than three years in prison; 50% have served more than five years in prison; 20% have served more than ten years in prison; 36% have served at least two terms. When asked, 70% of the parolees reported that prison did little or nothing to prepare them for parole. Even after being released—something long awaited—the experience of reentry was negative for at least one-half of the parolees. Most of them have experienced failure many times before. One-third had gone through the cycle of prison and release previously. All have been caught and labeled "ex-con."

In spite of these past failures, the parolees express a high level of aspiration. They think they will "go far" in the next few years, and two-thirds of the parolees said they would definitely "make it" on parole; another 25% said they were pretty sure they would; only one said he wasn't sure. What are their chances? They are released with less than $50, and 40% are unemployed. Only a few have the emotional support of marriage, and 50% are not returning to the community in which they resided when they were convicted. In other words, they are not socially anchored. Their patterns of social interaction differ considerably from those of the general public; they are less likely to visit relatives and are more likely to rely upon friends. Two-thirds of the parolees grew up in areas where there was crime and delinquency and about the same number have known convicts most of their life. At present, only about one-fourth of them associate with convicts. This can be a healthy sign that some, at least, are breaking away from the group of "old associates" who might reinforce the parolee's tendency toward deviancy according to Sutherland's theory of differential association. It is not clear who, if anyone, will replace this void.

The most pressing needs expressed by the parolees were physical and material, including a job, money and a place to stay. The parolees' greatest concerns were that they were not using their ability, they lacked money and their education was inadequate. They also have social and emotional problems. The ex-felons reveal self-concepts which are relatively detached from identification with stable social institutions and relationships, and which reflect the unpredictability and rejection experienced in the post-release social world. Yet, the findings suggest that the parolees often desire to be part of the "straight society."

When the parolees were asked to suggest programs for their parole, some said they had never thought about it. Their thoughts revolve around immediate, obvious needs, a characteristic more likely to be displayed by the lower class and inconsistent with the middle-class orientation which the parolees expressed in other areas of the study. They usually had not thought about the reasons for their crimes, or what kinds of programs would be helpful. The most frequent program ideas were for material help, such as jobs or money. Several suggested the idea of a living allowance for some specified time after release. Others suggested the need for guidance, security and someone to talk to. Some thought it would be good to have an ex-convict, who was "making it" in the straight world, talk to them. Many of them are already working in some way to help other convicts.

The parolees seem to have certain middle-class values, and they usually compare themselves with the average citizen, and aspire to a job, house, car and family. The fact that their means are so limited supports Merton's theory of the disjunction between goals and means. Yet, for some reason not determined in this research, the alternatives chosen for reaching these goals have been outside of the law. A crucial part of any program of reformation should be to make possible other choices for the offender and make resources available which are within the law.

The basic needs of the man who is freed from prison must first be satisfied, because as long as he is worried about how he is going to get money for lodging, transportation and a razor, etc., he will not respond to counseling or guidance. Maslow has pointed this out. The offender must first have the security of a job or money as he looks to the future, or (because he is a proud individual) he is likely to do as one of the parolees said: "I would take up a gun before I would seek charity." A need for independence emerges from the interviews, probably because of the men's incarceration, but possibly because many are by nature independent. The parolees usually do not blame the system for where they are. However, if something goes well, they tend to ascribe the success specifically to themselves and if they are unlucky, the blame is often placed "out there" in an abstract way.

It seems, then, that the most successful program for the offender would be one which allowed him to feel "like a man," and to be self-sufficient. He needs to have his ego rebuilt upon his release; the prison system has torn it down through coercion, control and humiliation. He needs to regain his confidence *legitimately*, not a false or imagined self-confidence typified by unrealistic expectations about his ability and future.

As the parolee reenters society, he needs someone to talk to, a successful ex-offender, for example. Criminologists, practitioners, and the American public do not have to understand very much about the parolee or the causes of crime in order to take positive steps to help him. Quite simply, his physical needs must first be met. As one parolee said: "It just doesn't seem fair to give the convict such a little money and tell him to make it." What "regular citizen" today can set out in the world, with less than a high school education, no job, $50, and no close ties or other resources, and "make it?" That is what we are asking the parolee to do, and we will not let him forget that he is an "outsider." He has affronted society with his crime, so he is labeled an ex-convict, which makes it less likely that he can obtain employment. Yet, according to Becker (1963: 31), if he had a conventional job or a reputation to maintain, he would be less likely to be deviant.

The parolees were asked to talk about their needs, and they

have said it best:

> *Let the fact that you're caught, convicted and sent there be punishment, and then spend the time in prison preparing the guy to be a good citizen when he gets out. Don't punish him all the time he's in.*
>
> *San Diego Parolee, 1970*

. . . or after he is released.

Chapter 9

# Recommendations

## Recommendations From Parole*

Marital and other family relationships should be maintained while the inmate is serving time in prison. Parolees seem to do better when they have a wife and family (social ties).

The offenders need to have their civil and legal rights explained to them by an attorney while they are in prison and upon release. Too often, because of a distorted orientation, the parolee does not understand, for example, that he can find relief from past and present debts. He then runs from responsibilities out of fear.

College as a parole plan, with adequate subsistence, is an excellent idea for certain parolees. As long as a parolee's education is below average, so is his employment potential.

Programs, both in and out of prison, designed to change the offender's ideas and lifestyles and to motivate him, reeducate him, give him job training and job skills, are essential to the reduction of crime. Change must be toward motivation, not punishment.

Community resources should be mobilized to meet the needs of the offender upon his release. These should include, at the least, vocational rehabilitation services, lodging, peer-group counseling, and non-punitive assistance.

The parole agents should have reasonable caseloads so that they may effect change. Some caseloads are 90 or 95, with 15 pre-

*Mr. Paul O. Cossette, District Administrator of Parole and Community Service Division, California Department of Corrections, San Diego, California.

parolees, which precludes the possibility of any real assistance to the parolee.

The parolee should be released with an amount of money that would give him a fair chance of making his adjustment. Approximately $3,500 a year is spent to keep an individual in prison; yet he is released with less than $50 and expected to succeed.

Community treatment should precede any notion of being sent to prison. Whenever possible, and with reasonable safety to the community, the offender should be kept in the community instead of being sent to prison. The prison is an unnatural and destructive setting which usually does not change the inmate, or make him less likely to commit crimes.

### Recommendations From Rehabilitation*

The objective of a rehabilitation program for parolees should be to create a lifestyle plan. Such a "habilitation" program should be encompassing and include physical, social and psychological components such as time-structuring, social relationships, education, job training and placement, which can lead the offender to becoming socially anchored.

An allowance for basic living expenses is crucial for the offender upon his release. He should have the autonomy to manage these finances and the responsibility for them.

It is necessary to have a person whose primary concern is for the individual offender who can work with him. This worker's primary charge should be meeting the needs of the individual, rather than the needs of any particular agency. It is essential that this person *not* be connected with law enforcement.

A decision-making climate should be created for the offender, with options for allocating his resources, however limited, so that he may be responsible for making his own decisions and plans for his rehabilitation program.

---

*Mr. Christopher Minard, District Administrator, California Department of Rehabilitation, San Diego, California.
Mr. Eugene Bischoff, Rehabilitation Supervisor, California Department of Rehabilitation, San Diego, California.
Mr. Don Sayre, Rehabilitation Supervisor, California Department of Rehabilitation, San Diego, California.

A multi-service center for offenders—a community correctional center— is appropriate for moving offenders toward a tie with the larger social structure, and toward meeting the gamut of needs of the offender, that is, physical as well as social and personal.

An educational or therapeutic tool would be useful for dealing with the unrealistic aspirations of the offender and enabling him to reach realistic expectations regarding himself and his environment without having to go through a long series of trial and error.

### Recommendations From Ex-offenders, Inc.*

In light of what we have learned from this study, and what we have learned from our incarceration in California prisons, while we were on parole, and while we have been working professionally in corrections, we—the directors of Ex-offender Resources, Inc.—submit the following recommendations:

Immediately upon his release the parolee should be made eligible for unemployment benefits as needed for a period of 6 months. The first week, the first month, the first 6 months—these are crucial times for the parolee and money for his support a crucial need that if met will do much to insure his success on parole.

Immediately upon his release the opportunity should be made available to the parolee for an on-the-job training slot commensurate with his ability and choice. The idea here is to afford him opportunity to become self-supporting as soon as possible and to begin preparation for a meaningful life task.

Full educational and vocational opportunity commensurate with his ability and choice should be made available to the parolee so that he can continue and complete his preparation for a career that will afford him long-term satisfaction and advancement possibilities.

Small self-governed residential centers should be established to meet the needs of parolees who have no family or place to go when released from a correctional institution. In the early months of their parole, there is an acute need for these parolees to share a living arrangement with peers with whom they share a common

---

*Mr. Archie V. Connett, Mr. Ray Johnson, and Mr. Robert McKinney.

experience and language and feel at home.

An arrangement should be devised in which a parole agent, a vocational counselor, and other professionals with agencies, programs, and services (legal, medical, dental, counseling, etc.) are brought into a close working relationship with parolees living either in or outside the residential center, in order to utilize these resources more effectively and economically in meeting the needs of parolees.

Immediately upon his release the parolee should be encouraged to join an organized self-help group comprised of peers (parolees and ex-parolees) and community volunteers (selected, trained and supervised by professionals). The new parolee needs to relate to and consider his problems with not only the peer with whom he feels comfortable but also the able, community volunteer. The volunteer with his people skills and knowledge of community resources—of agencies, programs, and services—the volunteer he can identify with and look to in time of trouble, can help him construct a bridge over which he can cross to the community.

After six months each parolee should be strongly encouraged to volunteer his services in a self-help group for another six months—this time as a helper. This will enable him not only to help other parolees "make it" in the community but also to experience satisfaction from his contribution and to become even more socially competent himself. And, of course, this is a way of insuring perpetuation of the quality peer group.

The parolee should be permitted to associate freely with other parolees except where the agent has specific indication that association might be detrimental to the parolee or to the community's welfare. The parolee should be encouraged to associate with other parolees particularly in self-help groups and other constructive activities.

A systematic evaluative and research component should be built into the parolee residential center. This will insure a valid basis and direction upon which to innovate change as needed and eventually provide information upon which a model approach may be created that can be used in other communities.

Ex-Offender Resources, Inc. and other ex-offender organizations should be looked to and called upon as a planning, programming, and consulting resource in seeking solutions to the problems of the offender. (Ex-Offender Resources, Inc. is a new non-profit corporation comprised of ex-offenders with many years of prison experience who are presently working as professionals in corrections. The major purpose of the organization is to address itself to devising ways of meeting acute needs as they appear on the spectrum of the system of criminal justice.)

Ex-offenders should be strongly encouraged to make full use of the job-bonding plan currently sponsored by the Department of Labor and which is being extended to all ex-offenders who need to be bonded in order to qualify for jobs. Out of 2,300 ex-offenders bonded under the plan, only 30 have defaulted. This plan increases job opportunity enormously and full use should be made of it.

In each correctional institution a committee of inmates who know what is going on should apprise each new arrival of his opportunities for growth and development. The new arrival is still inclined to be apprehensive about and hostile toward staff; there is, though, good possibility that he might be influenced by his peers to take advantage of opportunities available to him to help himself.

The correctional institution should make a major effort to involve the local community in activities that permit a broader opportunity for healthy interaction between the sexes including appropriate conjugal visits. There is great need for life in the correctional setting to approximate as closely as possible that in the community.

Able volunteers should be located through the joint efforts of the correctional institution's staff and the local community and then trained to participate in programs designed to help the inmate and to improve staff morale and community relations.

The correctional institution should make more use of the 72-hour pass. People who are to be released on parole to the community need to be brought into relationship to it gradually—through what might be called a "stepping-stone process."

Ex-Offender Resources, Inc. and other ex-offender groups

should provide committees of ex-offenders who have been successful in the outer community to orient newly released offenders realistically to life in the community—its problems, programs and services.

# Epilogue

by
Archie V. Connett

For quite a long while now, I have been thinking about the needs of the offender. For quite a long time I lived in the private country of the criminal. On December 23, 1952, after a year of estrangement from my wife—in a moment of madness—I took the lives of my three small children and almost destroyed my wife and myself.

My wife and children were my little world. When my wife withdrew her love and affection, when she rejected me again and again, my mind and energy over the months, night and day, were bent on getting her back. When, after attempting to please her, waiting, arguing with her, when my wife said things to me I could not stand to hear, and struck me—when this happened, I felt cut off with terrible finality, violated, betrayed, almost inundated with terror. I could no longer contain myself. It was as though something burst deep inside me. I felt impelled to destroy and did.

While I was attacking my wife, the children came screaming out of their bedroom, and my violence was transferred from her to them. It was all over in a few seconds. The explosion into violence, the manner and means of it, what I did to myself afterwards (cut both wrists to the bone and severed my oesophagus with a razor blade)—these were not the actions of a sane man. Emotional upheaval had transported me beyond a focus of awareness that included rational decision.

If the ambulance had arrived a few minutes later, I would not be here. At the county hospital a team of surgeons worked hours to save my life and repair the damage done.

For five days, I was given private nursing care around the clock. I could do nothing for myself. My hands and forearms were bound on boards to protect my wounded wrists. A tracheotomy had been done to permit me to breathe. Only my mother was permitted to visit me. I felt strange and frightened. Every time I opened my eyes, a nurse was there looking at me, waiting to care for me. I began to mend, to want to live.

After five days, I was arraigned in Municipal Court and taken by the sheriff and two of his deputies to San Quentin for safe-keeping. The authorities at San Quentin, I was told, would be able to provide medical care and protection not available in the county jail.

My first night in San Quentin was spent in an observation room in the "psych" ward on the third floor of the hospital. A naked bulb above the bed burned brightly throughout the night. It was terribly hot. Frequently, screams shattered the stillness. Mutterings, ramblings and obscenities startled me from an uneasy sleep. Every few minutes an eye would appear at the peephole in the iron door.

The next morning, wearing only blue coveralls and felt slippers, shivering in the frosty January air, I was taken across the Big Yard, to the North Block, then up in the elevator to Death Row.

On the row, I was told I would receive the best care available in the prison. A doctor would see me daily. I would have privacy. I was placed in a cell—a few doors down from Caryl Chessman.

On Death Row, you are locked behind massive stone and steel walls, behind a steel cage that encloses the row, behind the steel-barred door of your cell. A naked 40-watt light globe burns 24 hours a day. The bull—the armed guard—on the gunrail looks down on you. The truth of your predicament hangs over you; fear crawls through you.

For several weeks, I was behind the bars of my cell until my mother retained a lawyer who had me transferred to the county jail, a 102-year-old structure in which a corridor ran around a small cell block.

Each day, I was allowed to walk in the corridor, but at night I was locked in a small cell with three other men behind the solid iron door—solid save for a peephole. In the cell was the usual naked 40-watt light globe, two double-decker beds, and a 5-gallon can (a honey bucket). Outside, men lined the corridor floor, trying to sleep—coughing, hacking, spitting. All day long and a good part of the night, music and announcements blared forth from a squawky overhead loudspeaker. During the day, the population moved restlessly around the tank, talked incessantly, gambled. There were fights and attempted suicides.

After five months, I went to trial. There, after a month-long trial, the jury found me guilty of three counts of murder in the second degree and one count of assault with intent to commit murder.

The judge sentenced me to San Quentin Prison for the maximum sentence he could hand down: three 5-to-life sentences and one 1-to-14 to run consecutively. This meant 16 years-to-life. Later these sentences were aggregated by state law to 10-to-life, which meant I became eligible for parole in 3 years and 4 months.

In my first two years at San Quentin, I just put one foot in front of the other. The betting on the Big Yard was that I would commit suicide in the first year. Nights—after a hard workout in the gym on the top floor of an old building down in the alley—when I came out on the fire escape and looked five floors down to the pavement, it would have been very easy to have stepped off.

It was not until I was transferred to the California Medical Facility at Vacaville that I began to find myself. There I had five years of individual and group therapy. Therapy there was much like that at Synanon—hard-driving, uncovering. For months I had diarrhea and difficulty in sleeping. But I learned some things.

I learned that quite early my mother communicated to me an unstated proposal that had far-reaching effects upon my life: "If you love me, you will do everything I want you to do because everything I want you to do is right and good and perfect; and if you do, I will love you above everyone."

She kept the promise—as long as she lived. Even after my offense she treated me as though I were a god. In her eyes, I had been perfect: I accommodated to toilet and eating and language training earlier than children usually do. I measured up to her moral and social expectations. I became the all-American boy—a scholar, an athlete, a school and campus leader. I became a naval officer, a teacher and coach, a devoted husband and father. For thirty-nine years I lived entirely within the law. I fulfilled her expectations and she kept the promise.

With no father (my father was beaten to death with a hammer when I was six months old) to rescue me in my most vulnerable years, my obsession (to be loved by everyone as my mother loved me) and my compulsion (to qualify for that love by being perfect) took root.

To feel impelled to measure up to and to please others—to be always "right and good and perfect"—in order to feel right about yourself is a terrifying and precarious existence, and when you fail—catastrophic.

My wife and children were my little world—the principal people between me and the terrifying threat of isolation, failure and self-doubt. Confronted with this threat, having no real identity, ridden with anxiety, dependent on those close to me for constant assurance of love and affection that would stave off anxiety and give me at least some feeling of self and security, it was imperative that I maintain my little world. I could not let it go, accept an altered version of it, or create another. I had to have it. I wanted, desired it so much that I struggled to obtain it until I drove myself beyond the edge of sanity.

In therapy I learned what had happened to me and why, and what I must do about it. I learned I could not undo or make up for what I had done and that no matter what I had done, no matter what had happened to me, I still had the potential to go on living, loving, and creating, and that it was up to me to do so.

I became the right-hand man of the therapist, something of an auxiliary therapist, and the lead man in the psychological testing section. I learned to administer, score, profile and interpret psychological tests, including projective techniques. As lead man, I located and selected the men who worked in the section and trained and supervised them. Incarcerated military officers, teachers, businessmen, doctors, lawyers (even a judge) wound up in the section.

I had staff library privileges and I read and wrote four papers which I presented to therapy groups, AA groups, etc. People began to come to me for help. I was asked by the staff to take a therapy group. At one time, I had three groups.

Suddenly, there were not enough hours in the day to do all the exciting things to be done—all the reading, writing, working with individuals and groups. I was on a new frontier—learning and doing things that gave meaning and significance to my existence; but I never did an easy day of time in prison.

In my fifteen years in prison, I refused to think of myself as a convict, an inmate, a number. I accepted responsibility for what I had done; but I fought tooth and toenail to maintain my identity as a person. Not all custodial personnel nor even treatment personnel were happy with this, and I never hit it off with certain higher staff people who were easily threatened by a competent person traveling without benefit of portfolio.

With these exceptions, I got on quite well with most people in prison. I got on with most staff people because I lived within the rules, with inmates, even regulars, because it was known that I never "ran to the man" and that I would help where I could.

For fifteen years, I was between a rock and a hard spot from which there seemed no way out. I had been tried and found guilty by jury through due process of law of three counts of murder second and one count of assault with intent to commit murder and sentenced to consecutive terms. I was given the maximum sentence the judge could legally hand down. However, after I had served eighteen months and was to appear for a parole hearing before the California Adult Authority, the judge wrote saying that if ever a man in the state of California had committed first degree murder, I was the man; that if ever a man deserved to go to the gas chamber, I was the man; that I should never be released from prison.

Each year the judge and the office of the district attorney held to the above view and reaffirmed it in a letter to the Adult Authority before my parole hearing.

That I did not do a day of easy time in those years in prison may also be indicated by a few excerpts from a letter to the district attorney:

> *I feel the full impact, the enormity of my offense. It was bizarre, horrible. I think no one feels this more intensely than I; and I cannot tell you the remorse, the sorrow, I feel for having taken from my children their chance to live, for having failed them, my wife, myself, and others. I miss my family.*
>
> *I loved my children dearly, and they loved me. But in a moment of emotional upheaval, of madness, I destroyed them. I must live with this and memories of tenderness with them as long as I live. I would do anything to undo what I did, to make up for what I did. But there is no way to undo what I did, to make up for what I did. I can only give now to others what I have to give, do my best with what I have from here on.*
>
> *I have done my best to find a way to go on living, loving and creating. I am going to continue to do my best. But the offender—no matter how hard he tries to, no matter how worthy he becomes—can only join with and feel he is a part of society to the extent other people are willing to identify with and accept him on a one-to-one basis.*

The district attorney did not answer my letter. Instead, he again wrote the Adult Authority saying his view of my situation remained unchanged.

In my letter to the Adult Authority, I said:

> *I understand the feelings of the district attorney and the judge, why they have done what they have; but isn't what they have done and are doing, if not extra-legal, clearly beyond the intended spirit and responsibility of their office?*
>
> *Next June, I shall have been in prison thirteen years—three times my minimum parole possibility.*
>
> *In the jury's verdict and the consecutive terms of the judge's sentence, in the reports you have on my conduct and rehabilitation, in the indication you have that I identify with our society's values and still feel I have a contri-*

*bution to make, and in the knowledge that I am in the least parole risk category and have served three times my minimum parole possibility—in these have you not full rational, moral, and legal basis for releasing me?*

*What sense does it make, what good purpose can it serve, to go on punishing me for what I did thirteen years ago in a terribly disturbed, irrational state of mind? What benefit can possibly accrue to those who insist that it be done, to those who do it, to me, to anyone?*

But I was not released until two years later, until after the judge's death (the district attorney died of a heart attack three or four years after my trial) and some friends obtained a letter from the incumbent district attorney saying he would not oppose my release and that he thought the Adult Authority was in better position than he to determine it. After having been shot down, denied, thirteen times by the parole board—in my fifteenth year in prison I was submitted *en banc,* that is, to the full board for parole consideration. After another six weeks, I received word I was to be paroled with a five-year tail.

On June 30, 1968, after more than five thousand days and nights in prison, I was released on parole.

Prison is something different to each person who experiences it because each person brings to it a different heritage and a different life experience. Consequently, each person responds or reacts to situations that confront him there in a different fashion.

My experiences in prison, I am sure, were quite atypical, yet I am equally sure I shared a good many common-denominator experiences with the others there. It is these experiences that I attempt to illuminate and point out the implications of in my paper, "The Significance of the Helping Relationship in the Prison Setting":

*Incarceration in the prison setting places a person in a terrifying predicament. He is left running naked down the street, stripped as he is of supportive relationships, personal property, licenses, credentials, his rights as a citizen. Certainly, he is stripped of those props without which most of us ordinarily feel we cannot travel; and he brings with him to the correctional setting whatever emotional conflicts, whatever personal problems, he has. Also, he brings a knife-edge awareness that he has become an object of fear and scorn and hatred in some quarters of the community from which he has come; that he has, at least temporarily, been excommunicated from it, swept under the rug some distance away. Consequently, he feels alienation, a deep sense of loss and failure, of despair, and not a little terror.*

*He is given a number, a set of blues, and processed as a unit, an object, a thing, into the life of the institution where impending always is the threat of harassment, violence, and rape.\**

The person who goes to prison experiences excommunication and is branded a felon. He experiences deprivation—loss of freedom, supportive relationships, heterosexual opportunity, personal property, licenses, credentials, his rights as a citizen. He experiences depersonalization—is classified and considered as a number, a unit, an object, a thing. He is restricted as to time, place, movement, and behavior. He experiences, in no small part, loss of control over his existence. He experiences the treadmill of prison life—the emptiness of the days and the loneliness of the nights. He experiences continually the threat of psychic and physical harm. Finally, he experiences, the longer he stays, the threat of psychosis.

These experiences typically do not rehabilitate him—they may induce him to agree to an unwritten contract to become more manageable, more controllable, more institutionalized. It seems certain they create in many feelings of dependence, inadequacy, unworthiness, guilt, self-hatred, insecurity, frustration, alienation, fear, apathy, rage, and confusion. Too often prison experiences make a person afraid to trust himself and others and create in him a distorted picture of himself and the world.

These feelings, this distortion of perspective, in the person coming out of prison intensify in him certain needs. (Other people

---

*Taken from *Collection of Papers,* prepared for 1970 National Seminars in Corrections (Adult Basic Education in Corrections), 632 pp. Pp. 101-102.

have these needs, too, but because they have been met or partially met they are not so imperative.)

How can you help a person coming from a total institution (from a quite totalitarian setting) take his place in the free community, achieve a more satisfying quality of life, reduce the cost of his rehabilitation and the likelihood of his committing further crimes?

The parolee, like everyone else, of course, needs food, shelter, and clothing. But he especially needs to feel secure from psychic and physical harm—not just to *be* safe from it but to *feel* safe from it. He needs to be able to communicate with others on an equal basis, to be able to talk with others and to be listened to. He needs to relate to others—to be understood, received, accepted; to understand, receive, and accept others. He needs privacy—aloneness but not loneliness. He needs freedom and opportunity to decide and do, to be, to grow, to contribute. He needs new experiences, as does everyone. He needs sexual, recreational, cultural, and creative satisfaction. And he needs a life task that he can invest himself in that gives his life meaning and significance.

To involve himself (at the level of his competence) in the planning, decision making, and implementation of new approaches to effect needed change in the system of criminal justice is at once a means of giving his life meaning and significance, of rescuing himself from his predicament, and of contributing his perspective.

The offender has a unique, a potentially valuable, perspective to contribute. He stands in relationship to himself as no one else can. Only he can tell us what has happened to him, what he feels and thinks about the experiences he has had, how he sees himself, his relationship to others, his world, and what his needs are. The private country of the offender is largely untracked and unknown. How can we hope to design and provide experiences that will enable him to meet his needs, to cease his predatory activities, and to improve the quality of his life until we include his perspective?

We must look—the time has come to do so—to the ex-offender for his perspective for direction for these reasons: Because he alone in the system of criminal justice has experienced its total process—law enforcement, the judiciary, and corrections—as an offender. Because in a good many instances his experience, his intelligence and awareness, and his education and commitment qualify him as a potentially valuable resource. Because he has had opportunity and time and reason to assess the shortcomings and damaging effects of the process and to contemplate constructive change. Because he has a special vantage point from which to work toward not only remedying shortcomings in the system and aiding offenders presently trapped in it but also of improving the quality of his own life and influencing favorably his destiny. And finally because he is no longer a captive of the system of criminal justice, of any segment of it, or any similar system outside it—because in a few rare instances he occupies a condition of hard-won freedom (emotional, intellectual and spiritual) in which he is free to meditate, from the matrix of his own experience, upon the problems of crime and delinquency, the social milieu from which they spring, the system derived to deal with them: a condition of freedom in which he is free to think, to imagine, to make the creative leap to new assumptions and conclusions upon which new approaches can be designed that hold the promise of effecting significant change in the system of criminal justice.

*On June 30, 1968, Archie V. Connett was released on parole after serving fifteen years in five California penal institutions. He was released from parole on August 24, 1970. The day after he left prison he began work at the Western Behavioral Sciences Institute.*

*He has been an extremely valuable resource in bringing the perspective of the ex-offender to bear upon the problems of the system of criminal justice. He has contributed substantially to the conception, design, and implementation of this study; as a correctional counselor for the San Diego County Department of Honor Camps; as an instructor of "The Prison Community" at San Diego State College; as a speaker at schools, colleges, service clubs, the California Rehabilitation Center, the Riverside County Probation Department, the California Department of Rehabilitation, and the Criminal Law Section of the local chapter of the California Bar Association; as a member of three major committees in corrections; as a member of the board of directors of three organizations, including the local chapter of the California Parole, Probation, and Correctional Association; as a participant at local, state, and national planning conferences; as a consultant to the National Seminars in Corrections in 1970; as an expert witness in the penalty phase of three first degree murder trials; as the author of "The Perspective of an Ex-Offender" to the symposium, The Purposes of Corrections—Directions for Improvement, published in the* University of San Francisco Law Review, *October, 1971; as a participant on television and radio programs; and as president of Ex-Offender Resources, Inc., which was founded in 1970 to influence the ex-offender community to contribute to society. Currently, he is the*

*Executive Director of "Utilizing Ex-Offenders in Rehabilitation," a project at Western Behavioral Sciences Institute that has grown out of this study and is also funded by Social and Rehabilitation Service.*

# References

Arnold, W. R. A functional explanation of recidivism. *The Journal of Criminal Law, Criminology, and Police Science,* 1965, *56*(2), 212-220.

Axelrod, M. Urban structure and social participation. In P. K. Hatt & A. J. Reiss, Jr. (Eds.), *Cities and Society.* New York: Free Press, 1964, Pp. 722-729.

Becker, H. S. *Outsiders.* New York: Free Press, 1963.

Berzon, B. *Self-directed small group programs: A new resource in rehabilitation.* Final Narrative Report, Vocational Rehabilitation Administration Grant No. 1748. La Jolla, California: Western Behavioral Sciences Institute, 1968.

Bordua, D. A critique of sociological interpretations of gang delinquency. In M. E. Wolfgang, L. Savitz & N. Johnston (Eds.), *The sociology of crime and delinquency.* New York: Wiley, 1962.

Campbell, D. T. Factors relevant to the validity of experiments in social settings. In D. P. Forcese & S. Richer (Eds.), *Stages of social research.* Englewood Cliffs, N. J.: Prentice Hall, 1970. Pp. 116-132.

Cantril, H. *The pattern of human concerns.* New Brunswick, N. J.: Rutgers University Press, 1965.

Clinard, M. B. *Anomie and deviant behavior: A discussion and critique.* New York: Free Press of Glencoe, 1964.

Cloward, R. A. Illegitimate means, anomie, and deviant behavior. *American Sociological Review,* 1959, *24,* 164-176.

Cloward, R. A., & Ohlin, L. E. *Delinquency and opportunity.* New York: Free Press of Glencoe, 1960.

Cohen, A. K. The study of social disorganization and deviant behavior. In Merton, Broom, & Cottrell (Eds.), *Sociology Today.* New York: Basic Books, 1959. Pp. 164-184.

Cressey, D. R. Changing criminals: The application of the theory of differential association. In R. Giallombardo (Ed.), *Juvenile delinquency: A book of readings.* New York: Wiley, 1966. Pp. 467-471.

Davis, F. *Passage through crisis.* Indianapolis: Bobbs-Merrill, 1963.

Dembo, R. Recidivism: The criminal's reaction to treatment. *Criminology,* 1971, *8*(4), 345-356.

Gibbons, D. C. *Changing the lawbreaker.* Englewood Cliffs, N. J.: Prentice-Hall, 1965.

Glaser, D. *The effectiveness of a prison and parole system.* New York: Bobbs-Merrill, 1964.

Glaser, D. *Adult crime and social policy.* Englewood Cliffs, N. J.: Prentice-Hall, 1972.

Goffman, E. *Asylums.* Garden City, N.Y.: Doubleday, 1961.

Gordon, C., & Gergen, K. J. *The self in social interaction. Volume I: Classic and contemporary perspectives.* New York: Wiley, 1968.

Goslin, D. A. (Ed.), *Handbook of socialization theory and research.* Chicago: Rand-McNally, 1969.

Guilford, J. P. *Fundamental statistics in education.* New York: McGraw-Hill, 1956.

Handlin, O. *The uprooted: The epic story of the great migrations.* New York: Grosset & Dunlap, 1951.

Hartley, W. Self-concept and social functioning of former patients. Kansas City, Mo.: Greater Kansas City Mental Health Foundation. Mimeographed. 1968a.

Hartley, W. Self-conception and organizational adaptation. Paper presented at the meetings of the Midwest Sociological Association. Mimeographed. 1968b.

Holsti, O. R. *Content analysis for the social sciences and humanities.* Reading, Mass.: Addison-Wesley, 1969.

Irwin, J. *The felon.* Englewood Cliffs, N.J.: Prentice-Hall, 1970.

Kuhn, M. F. Self attitudes by age, sex, and professional training. *Sociological Quarterly,* 1960, *9*(Jan.), 39-55.

Kuhn, M. F., & McPartland, T. S. Empirical investigation of self attitudes. *American Sociological Review,* 1954, *19*(Feb.), 68-76.

Manis, J. G., & Meltzer, B. N. (Eds.), *Symbolic interaction: A reader in social psychology.* Boston: Allyn & Bacon, 1967.

Maslow, A. H. *Motivation and personality.* New York: Harper & Row, 1954.

McPartland, T. S., & Cumming, J. H. Self-conception, social class, and mental health. *Human Organization,* 1958, *17*(Fall), 24-29.

McPartland, T. S., Cumming, J. H., & Garretson, W. S. Self-conception and ward behavior in two psychiatric hospitals. *Sociometry,* 1961, *24*(June), 111-124.

Meier, D., & Bell, W. Anomia and differential access to the achievement of life goals. *American Sociological Review,* 1959, *24,* 189-202.

Merton, R. K. Social structure and anomie. *American Sociological Review,* 1938, *3,* 672-682.

Merton, R. K. *Social theory and social structure.* (Rev. ed.) New York: Free Press of Glencoe, 1957.

Salisbury, W. W. The self and anxiety. Unpublished doctoral dissertation. The University of Iowa, 1963.

Schmitt, R. L. Major role change and self change. *Sociological Quarterly,* 1966, *7*(Summer), 311-322.

Schneider, L., & Zurcher, L. A. Toward understanding the Catholic crisis: Observations on dissident priests in Texas. *Journal for the Scientific Study of Religion,* 1970, 3 (Fall), 197-209.

Schwirian, K. Variations in structure of the Kuhn-McPartland Twenty-Statements Test and related response differences. *Sociological Quarterly,* 1964, *5*(Winter), 47-59.

Shaw, C. R. *The jack-roller: A delinquent boy's own story.* Chicago: University of Chicago Press, 1940.

Shaw, C. R. *Juvenile delinquency in urban areas.* Chicago: University of Chicago Press, 1942.

Shaw, C. R., & McKay, H. D. *Juvenile delinquency in urban areas: The study of rates of delinquents in relation to differential characteristics of local communities in American cities.* Chicago: University of Chicago Press, 1942.

Shaw, G. B. *The crime of imprisonment.* Westport, Conn.: Greenwood Press, 1946.

Short, J. F. Dialogue. *Issues in Criminology,* 1970, *5*(1), 25-41.

Short, J. F. Differential association and delinquency. In R. Giallombardo (Ed.), *Juvenile delinquency: A book of readings.* New York: Wiley, 1966. Pp. 85-91.

Spitzer, S. Test equivalence of unstructured self-evaluation instruments. *Sociological Quarterly,* 1969, *10*(Summer), 204-231.

Spitzer, S. Manual for the Twenty-Statements problem. Kansas City, Mo.: Greater Kansas City Mental Health Foundation. Mimeographed. 1965.

Strauss, A. (Ed.), *George Herbert Mead on Social Psychology.* Chicago: University of Chicago Press, 1964.

Sutherland, E. H., & Cressey, D. R. *Principles of criminology.* (6th ed.) Chicago: Lippincott, 1960.

Tannenbaum, F. *Crime and the community.* New York: Columbia University Press, 1938.

Taylor, J. B., Zurcher, L. A., & Key, W. H. *Tornado: A community responds to disaster.* Seattle: University of Washington Press, 1970.

Thrasher, F. M. *The gang.* Chicago: University of Chicago Press, 1927.

Turner, R. H. Value conflict in social disorganization. *Sociology and Social Research,* 1954, *38,* 301-308.

Wylie, R. C. *The self concept.* Lincoln, Neb.: University of Nebraska Press, 1961.

Zurcher, L. A. The naval recruit training center: A study of role assimilation in a total institution. *Sociological Inquiry,* 1967, *37*(Winter), 85-98.

# Appendix

## The Population And Sample

As a first step in defining the population from which to draw the sample, descriptive information was gathered on all adult male felons who were on parole in San Diego County, California, as of August 5, 1970. The information was obtained from the California Department of Corrections, Parole and Community Services Division. The data gathered on the total population of 592 were as follows: 1) name, 2) address, 3) phone number, 4) age, 5) ethnicity, 6) length of time in prison the last time, 7) number of terms served in prison, 8) total length of time in prison, 9) date of last release, and 10) type of last crime. The parolees are described on Table 10.

From this population, a sample of 30 parolees was randomly selected (see Table 11). It represented the larger parole population on the major characteristics outlined above and is referred to herein as the "original sample," as distinguished from the "new parolees." In order to measure differences between those who have been on parole for some time (the original sample) and those who have just been released, a second sample was drawn from those who were most recently released on parole, that is, from August 24 to September 30, 1970. This sample of 30 "new parolees" brought the total number interviewed to 60. The "new parolees" and "original sample" do not differ significantly on any of the identifying characteristics listed above. The "original sample" had been on parole an average of 2.1 *years* when interviewed and the "new parolees" had been on parole for an average of 1.9 *months*.

## The Interviewers

Six ex-cons served as interviewers—two black, two brown and two white. Five of them had committed felonies and one a mis-

Table 10
San Diego County Parolee Population, August 5, 1970 (N = 592)

| Characteristic | N | % | Characteristic | N | % |
|---|---|---|---|---|---|
| *Ethnicity* | | | *Length of Time in Prison* | | |
| White | 362 | 61 | *Last Two Terms* | | |
| Black | 86 | 15 | 6 months–2 years | 193 | 33 |
| Brown | 134 | 22 | 3–4 years | 170 | 29 |
| Other | 10 | 2 | 5–6 years | 99 | 17 |
| *Age* | | | 7–8 years | 50 | 8 |
| 18-25 | 117 | 20 | 9–10 years | 34 | 6 |
| 26-35 | 246 | 42 | 11–14 years | 30 | 5 |
| 36-50 | 174 | 29 | 15 years or over | 16 | 2 |
| 51-65 | 43 | 7 | *Time Out on Parole* | | |
| Over 65 | 12 | 2 | 0–1 month | 35 | 6 |
| *Number of Terms Served* | | | 2–6 months | 184 | 32 |
| 1 | 381 | 64 | 7–11 months | 83 | 14 |
| 2 | 113 | 19 | 1–2 years | 241 | 40 |
| 3 | 46 | 8 | 3–4 years | 35 | 6 |
| 4 | 34 | 5 | 5 years and over | 14 | 2 |
| 5 | 10 | 2 | *Type of Last Crime*[a] | | |
| Over 5 | 8 | 2 | Against Property | 287 | 42 |
| *Length of Last Term* | | | Against Person | 182 | 27 |
| 1–2 years | 267 | 45 | Against Public Decency | 35 | 5 |
| 3–4 years | 186 | 32 | Sale or Possession of Narcotics | 147 | 22 |
| 5–6 years | 71 | 12 | Other | 28 | 4 |
| 7–15 years | 68 | 11 | | | |

[a]Includes multiple crimes. Seventy-seven parolees were convicted of multiple offenses (72 were convicted of 2 offenses, and 5 were convicted of 3 offenses).

## Table 11
### Socio-demographic Characteristics, Parolees Interviewed, Fall 1970, San Diego County, California (N=60)

| Categories | N | % | Categories | N | % |
|---|---|---|---|---|---|
| *Ethnicity* | | | *Number of Terms Served* | | |
| White | 37 | 62 | One term only | 37 | 62 |
| Black | 11 | 18 | More than one term | 23 | 38 |
| Brown | 12 | 20 | *Length of Last Term* | | |
| *Age* | | | 1–2 years | 25 | 42 |
| 18–25 | 18 | 30 | 3–4 years | 19 | 32 |
| 26–35 | 19 | 32 | 5–6 years | 12 | 20 |
| 36–50 | 16 | 26 | 7–15 years | 4 | 6 |
| 51–65 | 4 | 7 | *Total Time Served* (N=23) | | |
| Over 65 | 3 | 5 | (If more than one term) | | |
| *Marital Status* | | | 1–6 years | 4 | 17 |
| Married | 17 | 28 | 7–8 years | 2 | 9 |
| Single | 21 | 35 | 9–10 years | 5 | 22 |
| Divorced | 19 | 32 | 11–14 years | 6 | 26 |
| Separated, Widowed | 3 | 5 | 15 years and over | 6 | 26 |
| *Have Children* | | | *Length of Time on Parole* | | |
| Yes | 37 | 62 | (This time) | | |
| No | 22 | 37 | 1–2 months | 23 | 38 |
| No Response | 1 | 1 | 3–6 months | 11 | 18 |
| *Education* | | | 7 months to 24 months | 19 | 32 |
| More than 12 years | 11 | 18 | Over 24 months | 7 | 12 |
| 12 years | 18 | 30 | *Type of Last Crime* | | |
| 10–11 years | 13 | 22 | Against Property | 27 | 45 |
| 7– 9 years | 16 | 27 | Against Person | 23 | 38 |
| 1– 6 years | 2 | 3 | Sale or Possession of Narcotics | 10 | 17 |
| *Employment* | | | | | |
| Employed | 36 | 60 | | | |
| Unemployed | 24 | 40 | | | |

demeanor, for which each of the five had served a minimum of four years in California state prisons. Their crimes included crimes against property as well as crimes against the person. Four of them had served more than one term. Two were on parole and one was on probation at the time of interviewing. Their ages range from 29 to 47. Four of the six were working in a formal way to help other ex-cons; one with the Methadone program at a local hospital, one with "College as a Parole Plan," one with New Careers, and one with the Honor Camps.

Even though they were all fairly well established in the community when the study began, during the four months of data-collection some of them experienced a series of crises which seem typical of those faced by other ex-offenders. For example, one interviewer lost his regular job, was divorced, arrested on an offense committed three years ago, and fined. Another was arrested and held over for Superior Court trial, and subsequently convicted and returned to prison on a sentence of five years to life. One could not find other work and in general had trouble reestablishing himself in school and in the community.

The interviewers were trained intensively by WBSI staff in interviewing techniques, many of which had to be adapted to this particular interviewing situation. Role-playing was a crucial part of the training and the interviewers were briefed on survey research. The interviewers were matched by ethnicity to the respondents.

### Attrition

Letters from the interviewers were sent to each prospective respondent. There was a general format for the letter, but each interviewer gave individuality to his own by using his own words, and style. The parole agents were contacted to update addresses of the original sample and alternates. They were not informed when a parolee was interviewed, although the parolee sometimes checked with his agent for approval to be interviewed. Without the cooperation of the agents, the task would have been much more difficult and some parolees probably would have refused to be interviewed.

If the respondent did not have a phone, he was asked to contact the interviewer. If the interviewer did not hear from a respondent in a few days, he dropped by the respondent's residence, or if the respondent had a phone, an attempt was made by telephone to set up an appointment. If this was unsuccessful, the interviewer periodically dropped by the respondent's house until he located him. The interviewer went to the home address at least five times. Then, if a person could not be found at the designated place of residence, the interviewer began tracing him by talking to neighbors, local merchants, bartenders, cardroom proprietors, or the interviewer's own "contacts."

The interviewers persisted in locating the respondents, and because of their efforts the attrition rate was not as high as might have been expected for the parolee population. In order to obtain 60 interviews, 87 names were used, as described on Table 12. From the time the names were obtained from the parole office until the interviewers were in the field, 10 of the 87 parolees were actually eliminated from the population to be interviewed, that is, 2 were transferred and 8 were returned to jail or prison. Thus, 77 names were randomly selected to produce 60 completed interviews, an attrition rate of 22%, only slightly higher than for the general population. (Up to 19% of the general population are not contactable for an interview in their own homes even with 5 callbacks, according to Campbell, 1970: 27.)

Table 12
Attrition of Parolee Sample
(N=87)

| Reason for Failure to Contact | N | % |
|---|---|---|
| Interviewed | 60 | 69 |
| Transferred out of county | 2 | 2 |
| In jail or prison | 8 | 9 |
| Can't locate/Absconded/Moved | 9 | 10 |
| Refused | 4 | 5 |
| More than five broken appointments | 1 | 1 |
| Don't know | 3 | 4 |

## The Interviewing Situation

The sixty parolees who were interviewed received ten dollars each for their time. The interviewers received the same rate of pay for their time. The interviews averaged one hour, with some running as long as three to four hours. They were conducted during September, October, and November, 1970. The interviewers were flexible about where to conduct the interview and were equipped to conduct the interview "on the run," if necessary, by using battery-operated tape recorders. Usually, they were conducted in the parolee's home, and alone whenever possible. Sometimes this was not possible, and background noise on the various tapes includes television, radio, children, dogs, parties, and heavy traffic, both airplane and automobile.

If the parolee was in obvious and immediate financial need, the interviewer paid him "on the spot" and the respondent signed a receipt. Other times, checks were mailed to the respondents. The interviewers were not insulated from the respondents' problems and sometimes found themselves working to locate jobs, cars, training, schooling and even potential friends for the respondents. They were not reimbursed for these additional efforts.

## The Interview Schedule

The interview schedule was in two parts. The first portion was an informal conversation between the parolee and the interviewer. For this, the interviewer was armed with a guide for general areas of questioning, e.g., "What was it like the first few days you were out? How are things with you now?" These were general questions which did not lead the respondent but focused his thinking on his experiences upon his release. The entire interview was taped. The second portion of the interview was structured and included scales to measure self-concept, personal efficacy, level of aspiration, differential association, retroflexive reformation, and background and socio-demographic characteristics.

A first draft of the interview schedule was drawn up after a comprehensive survey of the literature. The interview draft was field-tested with three parolees selected at random from the population of parolees, and then submitted to two different groups for discussion.

The first group, previously mentioned, was comprised of administrative heads of local corrections and rehabilitation departments, professors of sociology and criminology, and interested ex-cons. They were drawn together in a Collaborative Planning Seminar. This group made some changes in the interview schedule and suggestions for the interviewing. The second group to review the interview schedule were the ex-con interviewers. They translated the interview into modified "joint talk" and made some additional changes in questions.

**Data Analysis**

The structured interview was scored, coded, tallied, and analyzed. Chi-square tests, rank order correlation coefficients, and differences between means were administered where appropriate. Two sets of controlling variables were used. One was ethnicity (black, brown and white) and the other was length of time on parole (new parolee and original sample). The data have been collapsed and findings presented are for the total sample whenever there were no significant differences between groups. For the open-ended portion, an inductive method of analysis was used, accomplished by first analyzing one-half of the transcripts and then devising a category scheme for uniformity in analysis and ease in integrating and reporting data.

The approach used is that outlined by Ole Holsti (1969: 95) in *Content Analysis for the Social Sciences and Humanities*. In devising the categories, the general rule proposed by Holsti was followed: "That is, categories should reflect the purposes of the research, be exhaustive, be mutually exclusive, independent, and be derived from a single classification principle." The two major research questions answered by the transcripts were: "What is it like being out?" and "What would make it easier?"

The unit of analysis used was the "theme," a single assertion about some subject (Holsti, 1969: 116). For any particular category, the theme was only tallied one time. For example, when talking about what is needed most, "job" was only tallied once for each individual, even though the respondent may have mentioned it more times or in various ways. Therefore, for any single category within a question, it was possible to have only as many responses as there were respondents.

# Index

---

*Fictitious names given to parolees interviewed.

*Fictitious names given to parolees interviewed.

---

*Fictitious names given to parolees interviewed.